Lost Arts

LOST ARTS

❦

*A Cook's Guide to Making Vinegar,
Curing Olives, Crafting Fresh Goat Cheese
and Simple Mustards, Baking Bread
and Growing Herbs*

❦

Lynn Alley

🜨

TEN SPEED PRESS
BERKELEY, CALIFORNIA

W

♻

TEN SPEED PRESS
Box 7123
Berkeley, California 94707

Cover illustration by Julie Marshall.
Cover and text design by Sarah Levin.
Interior illustrations by Bonnie Engberg.
Some of the recipes contained herein have appeared
in the *Herb Companion Magazine, Cook's Illustrated,*
and the *San Diego Tribune.*

LIBRARY OF CONGRESS CATALOGING-IN-PUBLICATION DATA
Alley, Lynn.
Lost arts / Lynn Alley.
p.   cm.
Includes bibliographical references (p.).
ISBN (invalid) 0-89815-674-2 : $9.95
1. Condiments.   I. Title.
TX819.A1A4   1995
641.5--dc20   94-46975
CIP

Printed in the United States of America
1 2 3 4 5 6 7 8 9 10 — 99 98 97 96 95

Dedicated to M.,
with all my love

The author wishes to thank:

My friend Bonnie Engberg for her constant loving support and her beautiful illustrations.

My agent, Julie Castiglia, without whose sound advice and whole-hearted support, *Lost Arts* wouldn't be.

Mariah Bear, the best managing editor in the world, whose dry humor and quick wit have made the completion of *Lost Arts* a piece of cake.

Rebecca Pepper for a very thorough editing job, and Sarah Levin for a lovely book design.

My dear friend and neighbor, Helen Mildner, who willingly devours and comments upon every word I write.

Deborah Madison for her inspiration and friendship.

Beau, Crystal, and Princess for warming the hearth.

Contents

Introduction

LOST ARTS is a book about reviving the "lost" culinary arts that were once the mainstay of the home cook. These arts were born ages ago in the Old Country and were kept alive in the new by the Italian and Greek grandparents of my childhood. They connected people to the earth and, when well done, would add an indescribable depth to dishes constructed upon their foundation.

Even today, vinegar made at home is better than anything you can purchase in a market or gourmet shop. A fresh cheese made with raw milk is an unbelievable treat, and one that, when you have tasted it, will ruin you for life! Breads made from grains milled in your own kitchen have an indescribable freshness and complexity of flavor that cannot be obtained in any other way. They taste and smell like the materials from which they were crafted and not like plastic wrappers, spanking clean machinery, and the cushions of your sofa. The pleasure of curing your own olives lies not only in the moment of consumption when, coated with good olive oil and freshly chopped herbs, you pop them into your mouth in tandem with a sharp cheese and a cool, crisp wine, but also in the moment when they begin to give up their wonderful aroma to the first water soak.

In retrospect, I'd say my own "ruination" began in the 1950s at the tables of Sara Quanchi and Mae Gorman. Aunt Sara and Aunt Mae were my mother's aunts. They lived in San Jose, which at the time was considered nothing short of the sticks by San Franciscans. I remember happily our family outings to San Jose; they afforded me my first opportunity to eat "real" food. I remember sitting at Aunt Mae's bounteous table. All meals in San Jose were served "family style," with large oval bowls filled with mountains of green beans, mashed potatoes, corn, tomatoes, and what have you, all fresh from the garden. I remember my excitement the day Aunt Mae decided I was old enough to appreciate the garden. She took me outside and proudly showed me tomatoes, herbs, and, by golly, the very string beans which we were to have for dinner that afternoon!

This was the first moment I remember consciously registering any connection between the food on my table and the land from which it came. The food on my table at home came from the grocery store. But the food in San Jose came from someplace different, someplace special. It tasted different, and the very act of eating it was a special occasion.

Outside these forays into the country, my world was full of food that came from the grocery store. It was only years later, in the late 1960s, when I moved away to attend college, that the lid really blew off the can of my food world. I had the grave misfortune (now I was really going to be ruined) to move into a rented room near the corner of Spruce and Vine in Berkeley, California. Spruce and Vine in Berkeley, California, may mean nothing to you. But just around the corner, at Shattuck and Vine, a young Alice Waters had opened her now famous restaurant, Chez Panisse. As a special birthday treat, my boyfriend and I went to dinner there. We walked away whistling under our breath, "Man, that was some restaurant!" It was that same Shattuck and Vine, by the way, which housed Peet's Coffee and Tea, from which I still mail-order my coffee today, it being the best available; the same Shattuck and Vine where Sahag Avedisian opened the Cheese Board while "waiting for the revolution," and the same Shattuck and Vine near which Alice Medrich would open Cocolat a couple of years later. A veritable "piggy's paradise."

It was there that I planted my first garden. I remember with pleasure the first physical labor I ever really encountered, digging up a small plot in my Spruce Street backyard (a plot fondly referred to by us residents as "the back forty"), composting all my kitchen scraps, and planting my own wonderful vegetables. I made my first jam from blackberries that crawled over the back fence and apricots from Anne Padover's tree. I made a memorable pork and cabbage soup with cabbage and tomatoes only minutes out of the garden, and spent hours reading Rodale's *Organic Gardening* magazine and dreaming about gardens. Yes, Spruce and Vine ruined me for life!

After a number of years living and traveling in Europe (and if France won't ruin you, nothing will!), I came back to settle in California and had the time and wherewithal to pursue my interest in the "lost arts." I began searching for information about making vinegar, curing olives, and making simple goat cheeses. I found almost nothing. Only a few scraps of information here and there gave the curious home cook any clues to go on. So in addition to pursuing my own interest in these techniques, I began to teach others how to practice the lost arts. My classes have grown in popularity, as has the desire of the general public to know more about making things from scratch, and as a result *Lost Arts* was born.

CHAPTER 1

The Old Bat, or
How I Came to Make
the Best Olives Ever

FOR CENTURIES, humans have been curing and enjoying olives. I have to wonder why. If you've ever tasted a raw olive, you've got to marvel at the imagination of the first person to pursue the matter! Was he starving? Or crazy?

We will never know for sure, because the Greeks have been eating olives since the Golden Age. (Homer refers to the olive "berry" on a number of occasions in *The Odyssey*.) The truth is, the face of the Greek landscape had changed permanently by the fifth century B.C., thanks to human "ingenuity" and the olive. Plato lamented that Greece's "green meadows, woods and springs" had permanently become a bare, rocky landscape within the space of a few hundred years. In the sixth century B.C., Solon (who thought he knew a good thing when he saw one) decreed that olive oil should be the only Greek agricultural export. As a result, Greeks scrambled to replace the few remaining fibrous-rooted trees which served to hold the soil in place (many others had been uprooted to build houses and ships and to supply fuel for Greece's metal-working concerns) with the olive tree and its long taproot, thus allowing the top soil to wash away and denuding the Greek countryside forever. (You, like I, probably assumed that humans' disastrous effects on their environment were a recent phenomenon!)

That's the bad news. The good news is that, thanks to the Greeks, olive lovers around the world today have a plethora of good olives and oils from which to choose. France, Spain, Italy, and Greece are the main exporters of olives to the United States, while California is the center of the growing domestic olive industry. (The olive industry in the United States actually developed as a result of the efforts of one woman, Freda Ehmann, who in 1897 began canning olives on her daughter's back porch in Oakland, California. The olives were from her son's orchard near Corning, California, and the recipe she used was one given her by Professor Eugene Hilgard, an agriculturist at the University of California, Berkeley. The lye-cure recipe produced a very mild-tasting olive, similar to the "California ripe olive" of today. Due to Mrs. Ehmann's aggressive marketing techniques, the olive "took off" in gourmet circles, gaining in popularity not only in California, but in fancy hotels and restaurants across the nation. The industry suffered a severe setback when in 1920, 35 people in the East and Midwest died of botulism from improperly processed olives. With the development of new safe techniques in the canning industry, olives once again became popular.)

By this time, you may be wondering where the old bat of the chapter title fits in. Let's just say that she was a rather opinionated friend of a friend who, during a discussion on the subject of curing olives, supplied just the kick in the seat of the pants I needed by insisting that she knew how to make olives better than anyone else. Her smug assertion prompted me to go home and make the best batch of olives ever. I used just a simple brine cure and a delicious marinade of top-quality olive oil; garlic; lemon juice; small, hot, red peppers; some ground cumin and coriander seed; and a chop of fresh cilantro. They were eventually consumed within minutes by the old bat and her friends, who left me nothing but a slick, shiny, empty bowl and a satisfied heart.

Where to Find Olives

Most of the world's productive olive trees are found either in the Mediterranean area or in California. But no matter where you find your olive trees, harvest time is universal. You pick green olives in September or October and black olives in November, December, or January. The olive flavor will be a bit more fully developed in the black olives, but either green or black olives make good home-cured fare. Flavor in olives, just as in any other agricultural product, will depend partly upon the variety of olive and partly upon its growing conditions and locale. Be sure to pick olives carefully so as not to bruise them, then clean them thoroughly and begin the curing process within 24 hours for best results.

If you live in the West but do not grow olives on your own land, you have a number of options. You can sometimes find olive trees abandoned by a former owner on unclaimed land. An olive tree's life span is 300 to 600 years; there are still trees in the Southwest that were planted by the Spanish missionaries. Or you can pick your olives from an area in which they have been planted purely as decoration. (I picked mine this year from the unappreciated trees around a local shopping center.) If you live in other parts of the country, you can often find fresh ripe olives in the Italian or Greek markets of larger cities.

Curing Olives

In case you think there is only one method of curing olives ("curing" an olive basically entails removing the bitter glucosides that account for its horrible taste), let me inform you that there are at least three hundred different kinds of olives produced in Provence alone. Everyone has a different method for curing olives. This I found out when I began asking the older members of my mom's Italian community how to cure olives. Each rushed to share the family's secret for curing the perfect olive. And each is convinced that his or her method of curing olives is the *only* way to do it. I was inundated with unreadable scraps of paper, slightly shaky handwriting, and photocopies of ancient manuscripts, all describing the way to cure the perfect olive!

But let's make it simple. I've found there to be three basic categories of home olive cures. There is the dry salt cure, the lye cure, and the salt brine cure.

DRY SALT CURE

The famous French Nyons olives (tiny, black, and pungent) are salt-cured olives. They are not to everyone's liking, especially those of us born and raised on "finger" olives. They are a bit more fragile than the brine-cured olives, so you might want to make just a small number of them for openers. To dry-salt-cure olives, you must first find a clean pillowcase, then make a drawstring top for it. Mix the olives with their own weight in noniodized table salt, pickling salt, or rock salt. Pour them evenly into the pillowcase and cover them completely with more salt. You then need to put them someplace where any juice that drips from them will not stain. (Why not hang them in a tree?) Stir or mix them well once a week for four weeks (or until they lose their bitterness). When they are no longer terribly bitter, rinse them carefully and allow them to dry overnight. Then pack them in oil until you are ready to consume them. You may wish to serve them with a sprinkling of fresh herbs on top.

THE LYE CURE

The lye cure is a different story. As you may know, lye is a highly caustic substance that can burn the hell out of you, but it has been used to cure olives since ancient Roman times. The reason it has been used to cure olives, despite its obvious drawbacks, is that it does the job of leaching the bitter glucosides out of the olive more quickly and more thoroughly than anything else can. (The comparatively bland flavor of the California ripe olive is the result of a good lye soak.) Call me finicky, but I don't relish the idea of eating any fruit that has been thoroughly permeated with a substance that can eat the skin off the back of my hand! So I, personally, use and advocate the use of a brine solution to cure olives at home (described next). For the curious, the basic process of curing olives with lye is as follows. First you have to find lye that contains no aluminum. (Most grocery store lye intended for home cleaning use contains added aluminum.) You must then carefully mix the lye with water and soak the olives in the solution for anywhere from 10 to 30 hours. You can see the flesh of the olive change color as the lye solution penetrates to the pit of the olive. When the solution has thoroughly penetrated the olive, you must then dispose of it in some suitable manner and the olives must again be soaked in water, this time to leach the lye out of them!

THE BRINE CURE

The brine cure is simple and safe, and it offers the most plausible response to my question about who first discovered that the olive was, given the right circumstances, edible. I suppose it's possible that, long ago, some olives fell into a saltwater tide pool and stayed there undisturbed for a considerable length of time. Then one day someone, perhaps a housewife or fisherman, happened by and decided to give one a try. Much to her delight, the olives had become pleasantly salty and quite edible. No doubt, she then took some home to her humble abode and, to her even greater delight, was able to duplicate the process. People still cure olives today in some Greek islands by dipping a basket of olives daily in the sea for 10 days. When the inner flesh is dark brown, the olives are ready to eat.

To begin the brine processing, place your clean olives in cold water and change the water each day for 10 days. (I use large, plastic, covered buckets from a local restaurant supply.) Weight the olives down with a plate so they all stay submerged. No need to cover at this point. This will start leaching the bitter glucosides out of the olives. Notice the changes in both the color and the aroma of the olives. At the end of the 10-day period, you can make a more permanent brine solution in which to continue the process. Add 1 cup of noniodized salt to each gallon of water. Use enough of this brine to cover the olives. Change this solution weekly for four weeks. At the end of four weeks, transfer the olives to a weaker brine solution until you are ready to use them. The solution should contain ½ cup of noniodized salt to each gallon of water.

Just how long it will take for your olives to become edible, I cannot say. Mine seem to take about two or three months to really develop a rich, olivey flavor. The best piece of equipment you have for assessing when your olives are done is located between your nose and your chin. It doesn't cost much to maintain (outside of your biannual dental checkups), so use it!

Store your olives in the weaker brine in a fairly cool, dark place and keep them covered. A scum may form on the top of the olives, but according to my mother's Italian neighbors, this simply adds to the flavor of the olives! (One of my Italian sources swears this is the "culture which consumes the bitterness of the olives.") Toss out the scum and use any olives that look unspoiled. (A squishy olive is a spoiled olive.)

LACTIC ACID FERMENTATION

I'd just like to mention here, without going into detail, that there is a variation on the brine cure that involves letting the olives ferment in brine. The olives are left in a mild brine solution, where, just like grapes, they begin to undergo a fermentation process, enhanced by naturally occurring yeast organisms on their skins. (The daily changes of water during the first 10 days of the brine cure prevent this fermentation.) Active fermentation in warm weather (70° to 90°F is optimum) may take a period of 4 to 5 days (signified by the bubbling and frothing of the olives), and you need to leave lids ajar or your olives may blow a gasket. The lactic acid fermentation produces an olive with a "bite" to it. (Further information on lactic acid fermentation of olives can be obtained by writing to the University of California Cooperative Extension, Berkeley, CA 94720.)

Serving Your Olives

To serve your olives, I suggest you remove them from their brine and rinse them thoroughly a day before eating. Dry them off and toss them in a marinade of really good olive oil and freshly chopped herbs. Let them rest in the marinade for a day before serving, and always serve them at room temperature, preferably with drinks, a crusty loaf of bread, and a hunk of cheese.

You might choose to embellish your olives with one single herb, like thyme or rosemary. Or you might use a mélange of fresh herbs that go together well. (My current favorite marinade, for instance, contains chopped garlic, red pepper flakes, freshly ground cumin and coriander seed, some freshly grated lemon zest, and a bit of garlic-flavored olive oil—a typical North African style blend. A Provençal-style marinade might include thyme, rosemary, sage, oregano, and orange zest.) I would suggest that you start simple and then become more complex in your combinations as you find out what suits your palate. This is an excellent way to familiarize yourself with the contents of your herb garden and learn different ways in which to use your herbs. Maybe you have an old bat in your neighborhood who will gladly render an opinion on the state of your olives. And as my old bat once said, "If you have any olives left by the time May rolls around, they probably weren't very good!"

An Olive Menu

Green Olive Tapenade

❧

*Yogurt Cheese Balls Marinated in
Fresh Herbs and Olive Oil*

❧

*Green Olive Bread (recipe in Chapter 6)
with Olive Herb Butter (recipe in Chapter 7)*

❧

Horta *Dressed with Olive Oil
and Lemon Juice*

❧

A Greek Stifado

❧

Melomakarona

❧

Suggested Wine: Retsina

It seems to me that a Greek-inspired menu is the way to pay proper tribute to the olive! Although no one is quite sure where the olive originated, some have speculated that the island of Crete is its home. The ancient Athenians, of course, believed that the olive tree had been given to them as a special gift by the goddess Athena, after whom, in thanks, they named their immortal city. And modern-day Greeks still cure and eat more olives per head than the citizens of probably any country in the world today!

Green Olive Tapenade

OK, so it isn't exactly Greek! Tapenade is a specialty of Provence and is more commonly made from black olives. The name "tapenade" comes from the Provençal word for capers (*tapéno*), one of the ingredients. Although I'm sure the locals have been making olive paste for centuries (olives and the first vine stocks to reach France were brought to Massilia, now Marseilles, by the Phocaean Greeks around 680 to 600 B.C.), tapenade as such was ostensibly "invented" by a chef in Marseilles some 100 years ago. This is a basic recipe for tapenade, of which many variations exist, sometimes including a dash of Cognac, sometimes a tablespoon of mustard. It is traditionally made in a mortar and pestle, although a food processor will probably work as well. I have a rough Mexican *molcajete* made of volcanic rock that works beautifully, producing an unctuous olive paste.

½ pound green olives	2 large cloves garlic,
1½ tablespoons	minced or pressed
drained capers	Lots of freshly ground
2-6 anchovy fillets	black pepper
(depending upon your	Dash of fresh lemon juice
tolerance for anchovies)	Fresh thyme, savory, or
2 tablespoons olive oil	rosemary to taste

Grind all the ingredients to a paste in a mortar and pestle or a food processor. The paste can be as smooth or as textured as you like. Refrigerate overnight to allow the flavors to blend, but serve at room temperature. Tapenade is traditionally spread on bread, but it can be used as a topping for pasta or as an ingredient in a piquant vinaigrette. My guests enjoy spreading the marinated yogurt cheese balls and the green olive tapenade together on thin slices of toasted baguette.

Makes about 1 cup.

Yogurt Cheese Balls
Marinated in Herbs and Olive Oil

I assume everyone knows how to make yogurt cheese. You take some yogurt, hang it up in a bit of cheesecloth, and allow it to drain until it is thick enough to cut with a knife. This can take 24 to 48 hours, depending on the original consistency of the yogurt. The cheese should resemble dry cream cheese or farmer's cheese and should hold its shape when rolled into a ball. If you make your own goat's milk yogurt following the instructions given in Chapter 5, and incubate it at a slightly higher temperature than normal (I use my oven's "warm" setting, which is about 125° to 130°F), you will have a yogurt with a texture that is particularly suitable for cheese. Yogurt made from 1 gallon of milk will produce 2 cups of cheese.

Once the yogurt is thoroughly drained, salt it lightly, then roll little pieces of it into balls about the size of walnuts.

Combine:
⅓ cup olive oil
1 teaspoon lemon juice
1 or 2 cloves garlic,
    minced or thinly sliced
Freshly ground
    black pepper
Sliced home-cured
    or kalamata olives

Chopped fresh herbs such as rosemary, oregano, dill, fennel, or thyme (Greeks actually use a surprisingly limited number of herbs in their cooking; these are the most popular.)

Add the cheese balls, coating each ball thoroughly, and refrigerate overnight, stirring occasionally. Serve the cheese balls at room temperature with the Green Olive Tapenade and slices of baguette or crackers to spread them on.

Two cups of yogurt cheese makes about 2 dozen walnut-sized cheese balls.

Horta *Dressed with* Olive Oil and Lemon *Juice*

Greeks are not salad eaters in the same sense that Californians are. To a Greek, "salad" often means a cooked vegetable of some sort dressed in olive oil and vinegar. And the reason that a typical Greek salad with tomatoes, peppers, olives, and cucumbers doesn't contain any lettuce is that in Greece they are not in season at the same time. By the time the warm-weather crops (tomatoes, peppers, cucumbers, and so on) are ripe, the lettuces and greens are long gone. In the springtime, however, rural Greeks are fond of gathering all manner of *horta*, or wild edible greens, which they may cook and dress with olive oil and vinegar or eat raw in what we think of as a proper salad. Some of the greens that can be found growing wild in the Greek countryside are:

purslane	lemon balm
curly endive	chicory
sorrel	dandelion greens
black mustard	collard and beet greens
arugula	

I grow several of the above on my "back forty" and am fond of mixing them together with a tiny bit of garlic-flavored olive oil and a dash of lemon juice or homemade vinegar.

A *Greek* Stifado

The classic Greek *stifado* is a beef, venison, or rabbit stew studded with plenty of tiny white boiling onions. In my atypical version, I use chicken and add olives. I also use good olive oil for frying the chicken, and I just don't raise the temperature too high to keep from burning the oils. Please note the particularly spice-laden Greek bouquet garni! As with most soups and stews, this dish is even better if you make it a day ahead of time and allow the flavors to blend overnight.

1 frying chicken, cut up	2 sticks cinnamon
A bit of olive oil and flour for frying the chicken	12 whole cloves
	1 or 2 cloves garlic, mashed
	2 sprigs fresh marjoram
4 cups chopped fresh tomatoes	1 basket pearl onions
	1 cup home-cured or kalamata olives
½ cup hearty red wine	Cooked rice
1 cup vegetable or chicken stock	¼ pound crumbled feta cheese
4 or 5 fresh bay leaves	½ cup parsley, chopped
8 peppercorns	1 cup chopped walnuts

1. Preheat the oven to 350°F. Remove the skin and cut all the excess fat from the chicken. Dredge the chicken in flour and brown it in the olive oil in a large, ovenproof casserole or Dutch oven.

2. Add the tomatoes, red wine, and stock. Then make a small bouquet garni by tying the bay leaves, peppercorns, cinnamon, cloves, and garlic in a bit of cheesecloth. Drop it in the stew pot.

3. Lay the sprigs of fresh marjoram across the top of the stew.

4. Drop the pearl onions in boiling water for 30 seconds to loosen their skins. Peel them and add them to the stew.

5. Bake for about an hour. Remove the *stifado* from the oven and then add the olives. (To me, the olives give up too much of their flavor if you cook them too long.) Serve over a mountain of rice, topped with plenty of crumbled feta cheese, chopped parsley, and walnuts. (These toppings really make the dish, so don't neglect them.)

Makes 4 servings.

Melomakarona (or Phoenika)

Melomakarona are traditional Greek Christmas cookies. They are sometimes called *phoenika* because they are presumed to have been inspired by the ancient Phoenicians who traded with the Greeks. Traditionally Greeks use olive oil for their shortening. Many Greeks of today have adopted the use of butter as a shortening agent. Use one of the lighter olive oils, one without the very distinct, fruity flavor of the olive. Many commercially prepared *melomakarona* are soggy. If you allow the cookies to cool first, then dip them quickly in sugar syrup (do not soak them), they will remain far more interesting in texture.

3¼ cups unbleached all-purpose flour	Grated rind of 1 whole orange
1½ cups fine semolina flour	Grated rind of 1 whole lemon
⅓ cup sugar	1 teaspoon ground cloves
2 teaspoons baking powder	1 tablespoon ground cinnamon
	1 cup olive oil
	1 cup fresh orange juice
	½ cup brandy

SUGAR SYRUP:

1 cup sugar	6 whole cloves
1 cup honey	1 whole nutmeg, crushed
2 cups water	1 strip orange peel
1 stick cinnamon	1 strip lemon peel

TOPPING:

1 cup chopped walnuts
2 teaspoons finely ground cloves

1. In the workbowl of a food processor, combine the flour, semolina flour, sugar, baking powder, grated citrus rinds, and spices.

2. Pour the olive oil, orange juice, and brandy through the feed tube and process just until mixture forms a dough.

3. Shape the dough into a ball, cover it, and allow it to sit for half an hour.

4. Preheat the oven to 350°F. Take a tablespoon full of dough and shape it into an oval cookie, approximately 2 inches long and ¾ inch high.

5. Place the oval cookies on a cookie sheet and lightly press a fork into them for an imprint.

6. Bake for about 25 minutes, or until lightly browned.

7. While the cookies are baking, combine the sugar, honey, water, spices, and citrus zest in a saucepan and bring to a boil. Simmer for about 10 minutes (until the mixture is somewhat thick). Strain the sugar syrup and place in a bowl.

8. Remove the cookies from oven and allow them to cool completely.

9. Dip each cookie quickly in the sugar syrup and place on the cookie sheet. Quickly drizzle with chopped walnuts and ground cloves.

Makes approximately two dozen cookies.

CHAPTER 2

Little Green Friends, or How to Grow and Cook with Fresh Herbs

I REMEMBER MY FIRST ENCOUNTER with fresh herbs. I had gone with college friends in a VW bus from Berkeley to the Grand Canyon during spring break. We had big plans for a week of eating and hiking. Along the way we stopped for a tank of gas and a stretch near Kingman, Arizona. As I sashayed around the unpromising Shell station, a small, aromatic plant loaded with tiny blue flowers caught my eye. "Hmm. I'll bet you could cook with this," I said to myself as I leaned down and cut some for the evening meal. I had no idea what it was at the time, but it looked edible and the taste was vaguely reminiscent of something from a can on my mother's spice shelf. Good enough. Into the evening's chicken dinner it went and my meal was a big success. Thus began my career in cooking with fresh herbs, and thus began my introduction to my most favored of all herbs, the humble but ubiquitous rosemary.

Today, twenty years later, I have a profusion of rosemary (several different types), sage, parsley, hyssop, chervil, chives, marjoram, thymes, oregano, sorrel, and other more obscure plantlings just steps outside my kitchen door in southern California, and for the last several years I have given culinary tours and lectures at the largest herb nursery in the United States. And I firmly believe that the only time one ought to use anything from a can or jar to season one's food is when faced with starvation or when camping in Antarctica. Every supermarket in every large city (and many small ones) now carries a decent selection of fresh herbs. They are available to nearly everyone. But the dedicated cook will inevitably want to do what I do and that is—grow his or her own. Whether in sunny southern California or the northernmost reaches of Wisconsin, there is always room for a few herbs tucked into a corner of the garden or sheltered in a jury-rigged greenhouse just outside the back door. (For great tips on extending the growing season in any climate, see Eliot Coleman's wonderful book *Four Season Harvest*.)

Growing Herbs

Growing most herbs is a relatively simple proposition. Let's face it: most of them are, after all, weeds. They require little attention and are far more resistant to insects and disease than most other garden inhabitants.

Herbs smell and taste good, thanks to their volatile or aromatic oil content. These oils are formed in tiny glands on the surface of the leaf. No one is sure just how and why they developed, but they serve several observable purposes in the life of the plant. They act as natural insect repellents. Their strong flavor and aroma make most insects want to go elsewhere. They also serve as a repository of moisture for the plants. (Most of our popular culinary herbs are native to the Mediterranean region and thrive on warm, fairly dry conditions. Moisture is less likely to evaporate from the leaves of a plant on a hot day when stored as oil rather than as water.)

These aromatic or volatile oils develop in response to the conditions in which the plant lives. If you want lettuce, for instance, to be mild and palatable, you need to supply it with a constant and adequate supply of water. If you do not, its flavors will become too concentrated and bitter. Conversely, keeping an herb slightly undersupplied with water will encourage the development of full flavor. (The best thyme in the world is said to come from the very hot, dry hillsides of Provence.) Supplying herbs with an abundance of water may encourage showy but less flavorful leaves.

The soil in which herbs are raised must contain adequate accessible nutrients. Although most herbs are not heavy feeders, unlike vegetables and flowers, a sufficient supply of nutrients and a well-drained soil are necessary. This is especially true if you are growing your herbs in a container. The more often you water them, the more likely you are to be leaching nutrients out of the container's soil. You must, under these conditions, fertilize regularly to ensure flavorful herb plants. Plants grown in properly prepared soil (with plenty of organic matter added) should need only an occasional meal of manure, kitchen compost, or fish emulsion.

Since most of our popular culinary herbs are Mediterranean in origin, most also require full sunlight to reach their maximum flavor potential. Mint, for instance, will grow in shade or semi-shade, but will develop far more flavor if allowed to grow in full sun. Those long hours of sunlight force the herbs to develop a hearty aromatic oil content in self-defense.

Cooking with Fresh Herbs

When it comes to the delicate matter of which herb to use with what, the world abounds with statements about the "natural marriage of tomatoes and basil" and carefully planned charts pairing dill with fish. To me these fixed formulas leave the most vital element of all out of the pot—the element of soul! In the words of one of my heroes, "Avoid reliance on cookbooks, and let your goal be the progressive development of your own cuisine. . . . One who slavishly follows [cookbooks] to the letter will never explore one's own resources, one's own culinary individuality" (from *The Unprejudiced Palate* by Angelo Pellegrini). He goes on to refer to the garden as a "veritable arsenal of culinary suggestions."

One summer recently, I had a goal of spending a lot of time in the garden and hanging around home, to see just how much pleasure I could coax out of the garden without having to run to the grocery store or gourmet shop for missing ingredients that came from China or Indonesia or some other exotic place. I wanted to see if we could eat well using a few good pantry staples and the bounty of the summer garden, and, I must immodestly admit, my effort met with great success. I tried some new foods and combinations that I had heretofore relegated to the "icky" category and enjoyed them. And although I used some good garden-oriented cookbooks to kick-start my imagination, I relied mostly upon the garden as the source of my inspiration.

Many books have been written on growing and using fresh herbs. Most contain basic information on the history and cultivation of herbs. Many contain information on their medicinal and culinary uses. Some contain innovative recipes. But it seems to me that all have one great shortcoming: they are books! And you can't really understand a plant, or know its taste or smell, unless you're out there in the garden handling it day in and day out! My advice to you is, if you really want to learn something about cooking with herbs, go find a friend with an herb garden, or a botanical garden in the nearest large city, or an herb farm, and smell, taste, touch, and eat! Then go home and plant your own herb garden.

Having given you my personal opinion on the subject of cooking with fresh herbs, let me now pass along a few suggestions which seem to work for me.

Consider that cooking with fresh herbs is a bit different from cooking with dried herbs in that the flavors of the fresh herbs are less concentrated yet more complex than those of the dried. (Many subtle nuances of flavor are completely lost in the drying process.) My personal rule of thumb is that when using fresh herbs, use lots of 'em. Unlike dried herbs, they can rarely be overpowering.

Whether you grow your own herbs or purchase them from your local market, the conditions under which you store them can also affect the ultimate flavor of your creation. If you must store your fresh herbs, always do so in the refrigerator. The lower temperatures slow down the process of degeneration. And never wash them before storing them. Any water on the leaves of an herb will encourage spoilage. (You can always "wash" your herbs off with a hose in the garden the day before you pick them.)

Once in the kitchen, be sure to use a very sharp knife to chop herbs. (I often use a perpetually razor-sharp Japanese ceramic zirconia knife.) And make sure the herbs and the knife are quite dry, or you will end up with mush instead of fresh herbs.

If you chop your herbs in a food processor, again make sure that both the herbs and the interior of the processor are perfectly dry, or the herbs will simply stick to the sides of the processor and the blade.

Most importantly, fresh herbs should be added only during the last five or ten minutes of cooking. Their volatile oils will dissipate upon contact with heat, allowing much of the aroma and flavor to go up in steam, so they should not be subjected to prolonged cooking and high temperatures. The exception may be the herbs commonly used in a bouquet garni, those tough, resinous Mediterranean herbs whose oils may dissipate a bit more slowly. Add a bouquet garni no more than 25 minutes before the end of cooking time and keep a lid on the pot to avoid losing your aromatic oils in vapor.

Classic Fresh Herb Blends

Most Americans grew up with memories of little cans of dried herbs sitting in mother's pantry. "Herbs" were simply the homogenous dried green specks sprinkled on top of the pork chops. As a child, I'm quite sure I had no idea of the differences between marjoram and oregano—not in flavor (how much flavor can you expect from a can that may be older than you are?) and not in appearance. Experimenting with some tried-and-true fresh herb blends may be one interesting way to get familiar with fresh herb flavors and spark your culinary imagination. Here are some of the most common fresh herb blends.

FINES HERBES

Technically, the name "fines herbes" just means "herbs chopped up fine," but in classic French cooking, the term "fines herbes" has come to mean specifically a blend of chopped fresh parsley, tarragon, chervil, and chives. You can purchase a dried version of fines herbes at almost any grocery store, but be aware that chervil loses nearly all its delicate flavor when dried and that dried parsley, no matter how carefully processed, resembles nothing short of barn sweepings. This is a blend that should always be used fresh and should be sprinkled on a dish at the last moment before serving for maximum flavor impact. Just to get a feel for the flavors of a classic fines herbes blend, try a simple cheese omelet, adding fines herbes to it just before you fold it in half.

BOUQUET GARNI

This name, too, really refers to a technique, that of tying herbs up in a "bouquet" or bundle to dangle in a soup or stew as it cooks. The size of the bundle will depend upon the volume of food, and the actual makeup of the bouquet garni should vary according to the tastes of the region in which it is assembled and the type of food being served. The classic French formula consists of some parsley, thyme, and a bay leaf or two, but in Provence, you may find rosemary, a strip of orange peel, or a sprig of fennel in your bouquet. My favorite bouquet garni for Greek *stifado* (see Chapter 1) contains both herbs and spices: whole cloves, marjoram, garlic, peppercorns, and cinnamon sticks! Although dried herbs are commonly used in a bouquet garni, you can easily concoct one from the fresh herbs in your garden. Just use about three times as much fresh plant material as you would dried, and bind them together in a little bouquet with kitchen twine or tie them up in a bit of cheesecloth.

PERSILLADE

Persillade is a traditional Provençal blend of chopped fresh parsley and garlic added to any rapid sauté, with a squeeze of lemon, just before serving. (*Persil* is the French word for parsley.) The Italian *gremolata,* which contains fresh parsley, garlic, and freshly grated lemon zest, is its culinary cousin.

HERBES DE PROVENCE

Perhaps more than any other people on the face of the earth, the French seem to make particularly full use of the herbs growing in their own environs. Herbes de Provence is a blend of highly aromatic herbs that grow wild in the hills of Provence and that can be purchased dried both in France and in gourmet shops across the United States. You can make your own fresh herbes de Provence blend from your garden; then try them in the Provençal lamb marinade in Chapter 5. The exact contents of the blend depend, as I see it, upon who is doing the blending. Savory, basil, thyme, and fennel seed seem to be constants, while lavender flowers, marjoram, oregano, rosemary, and even mint are the variables.

My Favorite Herbs

Here are some of the herbs that, for one reason or another, I wouldn't leave out of my garden.

PARSLEY

Parsley is a member in good standing of the Umbelliferae (or parsley) family. This is one of the three major families in which most of our culinary herbs are found. (The other two are the Labiatae or mint family and the Compositae or daisy family.) Plants in the Umbelliferae family are so-called because their flowers all form in heads that resemble small umbrellas (think of Queen Anne's lace, carrots, dill, fennel, and so on). There are basically two types of parsley that are familiar to the cook: "curly" parsley and Italian or flat-leafed parsley.

Curly parsley is probably the most overused and underappreciated herb in America. A sprig of it often graces the grub at the local diner, but its distinctive, yet not overpowering flavor has many uses in the kitchen. It, together with chervil, chives, and tarragon, is a classic ingredient in fines herbes and in a bouquet garni. I love to chop a mess o' fresh parsley all by itself over just about anything. At my very laziest, I admit, I chop and sprinkle it over Campbell's Chicken with Rice Soup or Top Ramen. My rabbit (and the occasional tomato hornworm) nibbles it from the plant. My cats get it chopped up in their food for added roughage. And the neighborhood dogs get it in my homemade doggie biscuits. A more tasty, useful addition to the herb garden I cannot imagine. And don't forget that not only is parsley good as a garnish or chopped up on top of things, but it is excellent in salads. I have even, upon occasion, made salads of parsley all by itself, dressed only with a bit of lemon juice and some olive oil. It has plenty of vitamin A and plenty of chlorophyll (hence its reputation as a breath freshener). In short, I always feel you can never have too much parsley in the garden or in the kitchen!

Just about every empty spot in my garden has a bit or border of parsley thriving in it. It isn't too fussy about its growing conditions: full sun or partial shade, plenty-rich soil, and moisture make the best parsley.

Many gourmet chefs prefer flat-leafed Italian parsley to the curly variety. I have heard its flavor described as being "more delicate" and then again as "more distinctive," "stronger," and so on, and it seems to me that each cook has a different opinion of the merits of Italian parsley. It is a beautiful plant in the garden, considerably bigger under optimum conditions than the curly variety, and it is well worth growing so that you can see for yourself precisely what you think of its culinary value.

Parsley is a biennial and its first-year foliage is what you're after. The second-year growth is never as lush, because the energy of the plant has turned to producing seed. My advice is to pull 'em out at the end of the first year. Plant new ones. Parsley seed takes such a long time to germinate that I usually buy little plants and tuck them in all over the garden.

CHERVIL

Chervil is a little-known star of the Umbelliferae family. The French use it all the time, but we Americans have yet to take this beautiful and flavorful little fellow into our hearts and homes. Chervil tastes nothing like parsley, although it is sometimes referred to as "beaked parsley" or "gourmet parsley." It has an indescribably delicate aniselike flavor and delicate, feathery green leaves. Chervil itself is a fairly small plant. It likes moist, shady conditions in which to grow and needs to be planted fairly frequently because you will want to use it all up as soon as you taste it. Let me pause to explain here that dried chervil is particularly useless. Its delicate aromatic oils and flavor components volatilize during the drying process. So never even consider using dried chervil! You won't find it fresh in your market simply because it is far too delicate and perishable to withstand transport and storage, so if you want to try chervil, grow some yourself. It likes the shade, abhors heat, and likes rich soil and plenty of moisture. In short, it's a bit of a little princess. You might try sowing some seeds every two or three weeks for a constant supply, since it goes to seed somewhat quickly. (Caution: wascally wabbits love this herb. I have to hide mine.)

ROSEMARY

Its Latin name, *rosmarinus*, means "dew of the sea," and it was probably so named because the best of it is said to grow on the hills overlooking the Mediterranean. It was, like most herbs, probably used as a medicine long before it was added to the stew pot. Pliny recommended it for failing eyesight and says it grows "in places with a good deal of dew." It has long been a symbol of fidelity and remembrance and as such has played a ceremonial role in both weddings and funerals. The ancient Egyptians placed bunches of rosemary in their tombs, and the Romans placed sprigs of it in the hands of their dead. I myself, being an avowed animal lover, have buried many a neighborhood animal companion in a bed lined with a cushion of rosemary.

Rosemary is probably my favorite herb, my "signature" herb. It was the first herb I ever bought, from a gypsy wagon at a Renaissance Pleasure Faire when I was 20. I took it home and set it in my window and nursed it along and used its fragrant needles to garnish a fresh poached egg each morning. (I called it an omelet—obviously I didn't really know what an omelet was.) Since that time, I have had a rosemary plant as a "pet" nearly everywhere I have lived, kept in either a pot or the ground.

Rosemary plants fall into two general categories: prostrates and uprights. The prostrate varieties tend to have stems that are pliable and leaves that are more plump and tender. For this reason, I like to use long strands of prostrate rosemary for garnishing large plates of food and for weaving little napkin-ring wreaths (or wreaths for wine bottles). The upright varieties have stems that are really sticks. One of the neat things you can do with them (an old Tuscan trick) is to strip the foliage off of one end of a stick that is about 14 inches long and skewer shrimp, chicken, or lamb on it. Leave the foliage on one end for decoration, then quickly grill your meats over an open fire. This makes an attractive presentation. Most varieties of rosemary taste the same, the more important variable in producing flavor being (as with most herbs) where and how the plant was grown.

Elizabeth David, the well-known authority on English and provincial French cooking, surprisingly pans rosemary as belonging to that category of highly suspicious aromatic plants used by Italians. She says, and I quote, "Many Italians stuff joints of lamb and pork almost to bursting with rosemary, and the result is perfectly awful." How very British an opinion!

Rosemary seems to be hardy down to about 15°F and is generally brought indoors in climates that endure harsh winters. It is a plant of the field and, of course, prefers full sun. It will grow in a more shady location, but will more than likely fail to produce its beautiful azure blue flowers. Yellow leaves signify nutrient deficiencies or underwatering problems, while brown leaf tips signify overwatering. The only real garden pest to bother the rosemary plant is the dog. Imagine my chagrin one night when I walked my friends outside to their car after a lovely dinner of roast chicken stuffed with rosemary. We stopped our conversation midstream (pardon the pun) and watched in horror as a neighborhood pooch "blessed" the rosemary plant from which our dinner had been taken!

THE ALLIUM FAMILY: GARLIC, SHALLOTS, AND CHIVES

There is garlic, the "stinking rose," about which volumes have been written; the elitist and not-so-well-known shallots; and chives, of which, like parsley, you can never have too much. Technically, all are members of the larger lily family: Liliaceae. And all of them like a good, humus-rich soil with a consistent supply of moisture. (The better the soil, the bigger the bulbs.)

Garlic and shallots can be grown much in the same way. First of all, you want to obtain some good "sets" of bulbs to plant. Then you want to place them in the ground, pointy end up. (The pointy end is the end from which the green shoots will eventually spring up.) Give them plenty of room. If you crowd them, the bulbs will be smaller than you may like. Before planting, always try to prepare the soil for your garlic and shallots with plenty of garden compost. It's best to plant garlic and shallots in the fall. This gives them several months of cold weather to get acclimated in the ground; they won't begin to grow until springtime. They will still sprout and grow if you plant them in the spring, but the heads may not be quite as large. In either case, set them out in full sun and rich soil and make sure they have a consistent, adequate supply of moisture with good drainage so they don't rot. They will grow all spring and summer and are ready to harvest when their tops turn brown and begin to die back. (In central California, most notably Gilroy, this happens in June or July and occasions the popular Gilroy Garlic Festival.)

Garlic has a nice, strong flavor and has been much prized in both cooking and medicine for centuries. I attended school at UC Berkeley in the late 1960s, when the "back to nature" movement was young and virile, and can vividly recall the pleasure of sitting next to someone for three hours who, in an effort to ward off a bad cold, was chewing raw garlic! There's no question in my mind why it was named the stinking rose.

When cooking with garlic, be careful never to burn the garlic because it turns bitter. Always add it after the onions, which take longer to cook. Also, the more you pulverize the garlic clove, the more of its pungent flavor and aroma you liberate. Pressing a clove of garlic releases the greatest amount of flavor, mincing it also releases plenty of flavor, chopping coarsely releases a bit less and so on.

Chive plants make a great border, with their cheerful little purple pom-pom flowers, as well as being a welcome addition to so many different dishes. They are easy to grow and, like their cousins, garlic and shallots, love a rich soil and a consistent supply of moisture. I like to interplant them with the parsley in my own garden because they seem to enjoy much the same conditions and do well together. You can chop and eat the leaves of the chive plant (as we all well know from our baked potato days), but did you know that the flowers are also edible? They can be used as a garnish or in salads, either whole or divided into their individual blossoms, and are just as flavorful as the leaves, and far more colorful.

Society garlic, *Tulbaghia violacea,* is not really garlic at all, but I include it in this section because of its similarity to the members of the allium clan. It produces no edible root and is grown mainly for its pale lavender, edible flowers and for its beauty in a border. The flowers taste very distinctly of garlic, yet are not overpowering. They can be sprinkled individually as a garnish over a salad, soup, or other dish to which you'd like to add a hint of garlic and a touch of lavender.

THYME

Thyme is a hardy, fairly drought resistant perennial, native to the Mediterranean region, which remains evergreen in all but the harshest of climates. Ancient Egyptians called it *thum* and used it for embalming purposes. To the ancient Greeks, it was a symbol of courage, and its name may have come from the Greek word *thumos,* meaning "courage." Medieval knights also considered it an herb of courage, often using thyme as a symbol of bravery and courage in battle. They say that the medieval emblem of the honeybee hovering over a sprig of thyme was meant to symbolize that the bravery of a knight need not rule out sweetness of character. What a great idea!

Thyme has been valued by farmers and beekeepers for centuries for its role in attracting bees. The most highly prized honey of the ancient world was the honey from bees fed on the wild thyme plants of Mt. Hymettus in Greece. Even today, thyme is planted on the ground of an orchard to attract bees, which then pollinate the fruit trees. Sheep and goats are set to graze upon fields of wild thyme to flavor both their milk (and subsequently cheese) and their meat.

Thyme has long been valued in herbal medicine, largely due to the merits of a prime constituent of its volatile oil, thymol. Thymol is recognized as a powerful antiseptic and was used as such on the battlefields of World War I, when more modern antiseptics were unavailable. The smell of thyme has always reminded me of the smell of my mother's medicine cabinet, for some reason. In retrospect, I think it may be because there was always a large bottle of Listerine at hand, and thymol is one of the active ingredients in Listerine, as well as in Vicks VapoRub.

Thyme is a hardy perennial. After about three or four years, the plants tend to become a bit too woody for cooking purposes and should be replaced with younger stock. Since it is native to the Mediterranean region, it appreciates warmth, full sun, and above all, good drainage. A friend who specializes in herbal landscaping recounts her interest in finding that the thyme plants that enjoyed full sun in front of her house were much stronger in flavor than those living in the partially shaded back. (Remember that herbs develop the fullness of their essential oils in part in defense against excessive transpiration.) If you are going to harvest or prune your thyme plants, remember always to let some leaves remain on the stems; otherwise you cut off the plant's carbohydrate supply and run the risk of killing it.

Thyme falls generally into two categories: the uprights and the creepers. In general, the uprights have all the flavor while the creepers make good groundcovers but aren't particularly bright in the stew pot, with the possible exception of caraway thyme (a creeper). One of the good things about thyme is that its oils are perhaps a bit less volatile than those of, say, basil. So they can be exposed to heat for longer periods of time. This is why thyme is one of the classic key ingredients in a bouquet garni. The leaves of the thyme plant are at their juiciest and most aromatic in the spring, just before the plant flowers. If you are going to dry any leaves (and I don't particularly recommend that you do, simply because all herbs are more interesting when fresh), this is the time to do it.

As for cooking with thyme, I can offer no better recommendation than that of Alice Waters, who says in her *Chez Panisse Menu Cookbook,* "When I cook, I usually stand at my kitchen table. I may pull a bunch of thyme from my pocket and lay it on the table; then I wander about the kitchen gathering up all the wonderfully fresh ingredients I can find. I look at each foodstuff carefully, examining it with a critical eye and concentrating in such a way that I begin to make associations. While this method may appear chaotic to others, I do think best while holding a tomato or a leg of lamb."

SAGE

Nearly every article I've read on sage either starts with or incorporates the saying, "Why should a man die when sage grows in his garden?" The saying echoes the medieval belief that sage was a panacea, useful for all sorts of ills and complaints. Sage's botanical name, *Salvia,* means "healthy" in Latin and reflects its favor in the ancient world. Hippocrates considered sage tea an important element in his pharmacopoeia. Charlemagne had it grown in his ninth-century domains, and the saying quoted above came from the famed medical school at Salerno, Italy, where classical Greek and Roman medical knowledge resurfaced in Western Europe during the tenth century, after a long vacation. Like most herbs, sage's fame seems initially to have been as a medicine rather than as an ingredient in the soup, yet it is to be found today in use particularly in the cuisine of Tuscany and France. The common culinary sage (known botanically as *Salvia officinalis*) is of Mediterranean origin and graces savory dishes around the world today.

Yet another group of sages native to the southwestern United States have recently begun to be offered by many nurseries here in the United States. Somewhere, way back when, the American native varieties and the Mediterranean variety probably share a common ancestor, but I'll be darned if I can figure out precisely where and when. The common culinary sages (*S. officinalis*) are milder in flavor, while the native American sages are far stronger in flavor and aroma. To my way of thinking, they are equally good eating. Some of the sages native to North America include California coastal native black sage, which grows wild on the hillside in back of my home (and which I often add to my breads in the spring, when it is plumpest and most juicy); the pungent Cleveland sage, named after the Cleveland National Forest in which it is plentiful; and the sacred white sage, which is not edible but used for ceremonial burning by native American tribes in the Southwest.

All sages clamor for good drainage, a dry climate, and full sun. Harvesting frequently will keep them bushy. Replace the plants every three or four years as they become woody. Remember that most herbs reach their peak of flavor just before flowering. If you allow them to flower, be sure to cut them back afterwards. Both the leaves and flowers of sage are edible, and the musty fragrance and flavor of sage traditionally have been paired with pork and poultry. Sage is a primary ingredient in the blend known as "poultry seasoning" that used to sit on a shelf in my mother's pantry.

TARRAGON

> We conducted an exhaustive series of agronomic experi-
> ments before arriving at the conclusion that, of all pot herbs,
> only tarragon and chives really enjoy an atmosphere consist-
> ing largely of exhaust gas.
>
> *William Wallace Irwin*

This amusing quote comes from Waverly Root's excellent book
entitled *Food* and is his recounting of experiments performed on
the balcony of W. W. Irwin's Paris apartment. I don't know about
exhaust emission, but I do know that tarragon can be a tricky little beggar to grow. It is a native of Asia and probably a hybrid of
some strain of wild Russian tarragon. One of the few herbs that
does not produce seed (the sign of a true hybrid), French tarragon
must be grown from cuttings. Which brings us to another point:
most herb books caution the reader to buy only true French tarragon and never Russian tarragon, which has no flavor. I had often
wondered whether or not any nursery was dumb enough to even
offer Russian tarragon until one day, when I was looking over the
herb section at my local branch of a mega-retail nursery chain. I
noticed a rather funny-looking tarragon plant. Being an herbalist
and interested in such things, I tore off a little bit of leaf and tasted
it. Hmm. Nothing. I scratched my head and then finally realized
that, indeed, I was standing in the presence of the legendary, taste-
less Russian tarragon. After some investigation, I found that the
reason some nurseries still try to palm Russian tarragon off on an
unsuspecting public is that they do not want to expend the time
and effort it takes to root cuttings of French tarragon. They can
just throw a few seeds into a pot, wait for them to sprout, and
then sell 'em. Make sure, if you are new to the world of tarragon,
that you buy a little plant that has clearly been "rooted" and not a
bunch of little seedlings in a pot.

Tarragon seems to need a period of cold during the winter, during which it goes dormant, in order to do its best. Here in southern California it dies back in the winter, just as it does everywhere else, for a little rest. Then, in the spring, just when it looks as dead as it's ever going to get, tiny green shoots poke their noses up through the ground around where your tarragon plant used to be, and voila! More tarragon! (May I pause here to mention that Thomas Jefferson, who was an avid collector of plants from the European continent, and who kept a garden diary for 58 years, grew tarragon at his home in Monticello?)

Tarragon seems most popular among the French, those lovers of anything that looks even vaguely edible, and perhaps its most notable representative is poulet à l'estragon, or chicken in tarragon cream sauce. Perhaps the most interesting tarragon dish I have ever tasted, aside from the tarragon Jell-O I was once served at a banquet, was a hearty lamb stew prepared by some visiting Soviet Georgian chefs. It was delicious! And I understood them to say that tarragon is much enjoyed in many dishes by their countrymen.

Mexican tarragon, although not truly a tarragon, is an acceptable substitute both in the garden and in the kitchen. It is native to this continent, unlike most of our culinary herbs, which are native to the Mediterranean region. It lacks the complexity and subtleties of French tarragon, but still has a distinct tarragon flavor. It is sometimes called Mexican mint marigold because it is, indeed, a type of marigold. It produces beautiful little bright yellow flowers atop its tall stalks and is much more easily grown than the finicky French tarragon. It will die back in the winter, but comes back vigorously each spring.

BASIL

Basil seems to be native to India, although it is particularly popular in the cooking of the Mediterranean region. The Italians use it in the Genovese specialty pesto, a mixture of olive oil, fresh basil leaves, pine nuts, and fresh Parmesan cheese, whereas the French have translated it into *pistou,* a basil and olive oil sauce often added to soups at the last minute. Although basil has played a role in Greek history (Greek physician/botanist Crysippos declared it one of his favorite seasonings in 400 B.C. and St. Helena is said to have discovered the true cross under a patch of basil), the Greeks rarely use basil in cooking today. It is considered more an ornamental plant or a deterrent to flies when placed in a pot on a windowsill. At one time, basil traveled as far north as northern France and England (where it remains as a primary ingredient in a classic English turtle soup), but its popularity receded somewhere along the line so that today its use is restricted mainly to southern France and Italy.

Basil needs, above all, warmth and sunlight in order to produce at its best! (Perhaps this is why its use ultimately died out in northern Europe.) Changes in flavor occur below 50°F, and the leaves and stems begin to turn black and rot. (I have been able to keep a basil plant or two going throughout the winter by placing them close to the outside vent for the clothes dryer!) Basil also does best in a rich soil, which is reflected in the color and taste of the leaves. If you plant basil in a container, be sure to fertilize it often for best flavor results. Poor soil will yield weak, yellowish leaves with a diminished flavor. Keep the flowers picked off the plant as the flavor changes once flowers appear and the plant's energy goes into flower/seed production rather than into leaf growth.

Some of basil's flavor components volatilize at fairly low temperatures, so basil is best added during the last few minutes of cooking. When, for instance, I make a four-cheese, three-basil pizza, I add the fresh basil only after the pizza has come out of the oven. To add it before then would mean the loss of most of the herb's flavor. Large basil leaves can be used whole in salads, and I often add a few sprigs of basil to a simple mint herb tea. My favorite way to use basil is to make a chiffonade of the fresh leaves and sprinkle it over any food that has just come out of the oven or off the stove. (To make a chiffonade of basil leaves, roll them into a cigar shape and then slice them horizontally into thin strips.)

CATNIP/CAT THYME

In 1597 John Gerard wrote that "cats are much delighted with cat-mint for the smell of it is so pleasant unto them that they rub themselves in it, and wallow and tumble in it, and also feed on the branches very greedily." Sounds suspiciously like he's been peeking over my back fence. You can count on finding Princess asleep under her favorite catnip plant any afternoon. And just watch the fun when it comes time to give the catnip a haircut! A bunch of dipsomaniacs at a New Year's Eve party never had so much fun. A fellow once asked for my advice. He hated cats. Did I know of something he could plant that would deter them? Easy—buy a bunch of catnip plants and plant them in the neighbor's yard!

Nepetalactone's the culprit. That's the chemical found in the essential oil of catnip that produces an effect similar to that of laughing gas in humans. Oddly enough, it must be inhaled to produce the "desired" effect; eating the stuff just won't do it. The response to catnip, by the way, is a genetically controlled response. Some cats have it, some don't.

(May I refer the cat loving reader to Paul Gallico's touching short story "The Secret Ingredient"? A French provincial chef/hotel owner wins a fourth Michelin star in a most amusing fashion.)

Cat thyme (*Teucreum marum*) seems to offer even more exciting possibilities to feline members of the household. Mine eat it, roll in it, crush it, rip it out of the ground with their teeth, and so on. In an effort to better understand the cat psyche, I tasted it and was surprised to find that it is hotter than Hades and bites back! I have since used the judiciously chosen sprig of it in my herb vinegar.

OREGANO

Oregano, beloved by both Italians and Greeks, and whose name comes from two Greek words meaning "joy of the hills," is highly adaptable. Native to the Mediterranean region, it has gradually spread into the cooler regions of the temperate zone. Much confusion seems to exist over exactly what qualifies as oregano, and it seems almost better to think of it as a flavor rather than a species of plants. *Origanum vulgare,* the plant most commonly sold as oregano, doesn't have a lot of flavor; *Lippia graveolens* (in addition to at least 18 other plants) is known as Mexican oregano. It is the so-called Greek oregano (which is botanically classified as at least two different plants) that is perhaps the most worthy of the American cook's attention. It has a good, strong "oregano" flavor and a spreading root system. This is the one you should buy for your herb garden.

Let me explain here that the flavor we characterize as "oregano," which is found in many unrelated plants, is due largely to the presence of an essential oil known as carvacrol. Almost any plant that has the characteristic "oregano" flavor is also going to have a high carvacrol content.

As for cooking with oregano, the Greeks, the Italians, and the Mexicans all love it as do the people of many other cultures. The Greeks, who don't have a particularly broad base of aromatic herbs in their repertoire, love their *rigani,* as they call oregano, and use it with abandon. I was once doing a cooking demonstration at a local Williams-Sonoma store, and I must have had some fresh oregano with me. An Italian woman who was watching began talking with me about oregano and how her family traditionally used it. I was surprised to learn that not only did they prize the leaves, but that the small, unopened buds were also used in their cooking. I have since seen it packaged so in dried form in gourmet cookware shops. (If you are ever going to use dried herbs, it is always best to purchase them whole and crumble them just at the moment you intend to use them.)

Both marjoram and oregano belong to the genus *Origanum* and their cultivation requirements are much the same. Oregano is the hardier of the two and can often be found growing wild all over Europe, while marjoram is frost-sensitive and may die out if the weather gets too cold. Both enjoy rich, light, well-drained soil and plenty of sunlight. Both self-sow and can easily be propagated by cuttings, root division, or seed. Three- and four-year-old plants ought to be thinned or replaced.

MARJORAM

I'm never quite sure just why oregano and marjoram are often discussed in tandem, except that they belong to the same family. They seem two very different herbs to my mind and palate. Oregano is rough and rustic in flavor, while marjoram is perfumed and far more highly refined, to my way of thinking. Oregano is a country lad, while marjoram is a lady of the first order. Marjoram was known to the ancients. Virgil mentions it in the *Aeneid*. Pliny gave directions for its cultivation in the garden. Both Catullus and Columella speak of it. And the clown in *All's Well That Ends Well* says of dead Helen: "Indeed, sir, she was the sweet marjoram of the salad." Its name comes from the old Italian city of Marjori in Sicily, which has a sprig of marjoram on an azure field on its coat of arms.

THE MINTS

As legend would have it, Hades, god of the underworld, was smitten by the beauty of Menthe, a lovely young nymph. Persephone, his wife, being apprised of the situation, quickly turned the young beauty into a sweet-smelling mint plant and trod upon her! Appropriately enough, mint has been valued for centuries as a strewing herb. In case you don't know what a strewing herb is, picture the floors of homes and castles in ancient times. They're dirt, more than likely. People chuck bones under the table for the dogs and nobody scrubs the floor! It's not a pretty sight. So to mask the unsightly odor and view of it all, sweet-smelling herbs were strewn upon the floor and replaced regularly. You invite somebody over to the castle or homestead for dinner, and you strew some nice mint or basil on the floor so that when they walk in, the mint gives up its delightful odor and everyone forgets all about the dirty floor. I admit, this may be an oversimplification— ancient Romans didn't have dirt floors and they used strewing herbs all the time—but this will give you an idea of what "strewing herbs" are all about! Ovid even mentions a hostess "rubbing down" her table with fresh mint because a couple of gods were coming to dinner. As a result of all these preparations with mint for company, it became a symbol of hospitality, both to the ancients and the medieval crowd. And admittedly, I enjoy nothing more than a barefoot romp on the dwarf pennyroyal that grows as a fragrant groundcover in my garden today!

Peppermint (*Mentha peperita*) is perhaps the most strongly flavored and aromatic of the mints. It has the smallest, darkest leaves and is somewhat creeping in habit. To my mind, it is the only mint that stands up to chocolate. This is the mint that flavors peppermint candy (surprise), crème de menthe, mouthwashes, medicines, and after-dinner mints. When you want a strong, obvious mint flavor, the kind that cools your mouth when you suck in, this is your mint! The most prominent constituent of its essential oil is menthol, the oil that produces a cooling sensation upon contact with the skin.

Spearmint (*Mentha spicata*), a kinder, gentler form of mint, is excellent as a tea, as a garnish, and in all foods where a milder mint taste is required, such as tabbouleh or mint juleps (nearly 30,000 sprigs of spearmint are consumed in mint juleps each year at the Kentucky Derby alone). Spearmint plays an important role in many Middle Eastern cuisines, and the Moroccans drink a strong, sweet mint tea. Spearmint is also found in some of the dishes native to Mexico in the region surrounding Guadalajara. The Mexican taste for mint was acquired from the Spanish, who in turn acquired their taste for mint from the Arabs. The primary constituent of spearmint's essential oil is carvone, so spearmint does not have that same "cool" effect that peppermint does.

Pennyroyal (*Mentha pulegium*) derives its name from the Latin *pulex* meaning flea, and it has gained some notoriety as a natural flea repellent. (For a while many pet stores were carrying natural flea collars impregnated with oil of pennyroyal. Personally, I sure wouldn't want to wear a collar impregnated with oil of penny-royal around my neck for very long. And I can't imagine any poor dog or cat, whose "smellers" are many times more sensitive than my own, enjoying the experience!) Pennyroyal has been more commonly used in medicine than in cooking, but Angelo Pellegrini speaks of *puleggio* (Italian for pennyroyal), an herb that his mother served often with frogs in tomato sauce!

Corsican mint is a tiny, shade-loving plant that makes an excellent groundcover in shady locations, as does dwarf pennyroyal, the groundcover of choice in my own garden. I love walking on it in my bare feet, and guests always seems delighted by its aroma.

Most of the mints will thrive in either sun or shade (dwarf pennyroyal demands shade, and pennyroyal prefers it), and all of them love rich soil with plenty of moisture. I find they do particularly well planted in the locality of a leaky faucet. Mints spread by means of runners and are usually wildly invasive. For this reason, I suggest planting your mints in a container unless you anticipate having plenty of time to keep them under control in the ground, which is almost impossible!

SAFFRON

Imagine my excitement as I unwrapped my first package of saffron crocus bulbs from Seeds Blum in Idaho! Saffron, often touted as the most expensive spice in the world, growing right in my own backyard! It seemed impossible to believe that I might be able to produce a usable saffron in my own garden. Somehow it seemed to me that saffron had to come from acres and acres of fields growing in the dry, hot climate of La Mancha (where the best saffron in the world is said to come from) and not from coastal southern California. Yet, one morning not long ago, I turned out my very first loaf of a Provençal saffron bread, and was I proud! Those beautiful threads of golden orange lending their color to the dough, and that wonderful, subtle, musty aroma intermingled with the sweet nuttiness of freshly ground wheat flour . . . mmmmm!

The saffron flowers themselves are breathtakingly beautiful—a rich, royal, deep purple crocus blossom with three deeply colored orange stigmata in the center. Each bulb will produce one blossom the first year and as many as five or six blossoms over a period of two or three weeks in the ensuing few years. (I quickly learned to cover my precious emerging blossoms with strawberry baskets in a race against Attila the Bun!) As for having to grow them in La Mancha, or any hot, dry climate, saffron was a good cash crop for more than four hundred years in Saffron Walden, Essex, England, where the little flowers were grown to supply the dyers and apothecaries of the day.

How, you might ask, did the saffron crocus come to England in the first place? Some say it was brought home by returning Crusaders in the twelfth century, while others claim it was brought much earlier to the British Isles by Phoenician traders looking for tin. The ancient Greeks seem to have been big saffron fans. Theophrastus wrote about the "saffron colored hillsides and roadsides of Greece" in the fourth century B.C., and the murals on the walls at the palace of Knossos depict the saffron harvest in about 3000 B.C.! Saffron is found today, oddly enough, in the cooking of the Pennsylvania Dutch in our own country, seemingly all the result of one family who emigrated from Germany, where they had been engaged in raising saffron, and who brought the "tools of the trade" with them.

Today saffron is a characteristic seasoning in French bouillabaisse, Spanish paella, Swedish and Cornish saffron breads, Greek Easter bread, some Indian dishes, and Provençal and Italian cooking.

An Herb Picnic Menu

Old-Fashioned Herb Fried Chicken

🌿

Iced Herb Gazpacho

🌿

Tarragon Potato Salad
with Homemade Garlic Mayonnaise

🌿

Cleveland Sage Country Loaf (recipe in Chapter 6)
with Patti's Industrial Strength Garlic Spread
(recipe in Chapter 7)

🌿

Chocolate Peppermint Fudge

🌿

Lemon Verbena Shortbread

🌿

Herb Lemonade

🌿

Suggested Wine: Pinot Gris or Pinot Grigio

My Herb Picnic Menu was originally designed for the culinary
herb tours and luncheons I did at Taylor's Herb Gardens in
Vista, California, which at the time was the largest herb nursery in the United States. They have a wonderful rolling expanse
of green lawn on which I spent many happy hours picnicking,
talking, and laughing, and an extensive "mother garden" full of
herbal delights and fragrant plants and flowers.

Old-Fashioned Herb Fried Chicken

One hot, sultry afternoon, while watching a videotape of Driving Miss Daisy for the first time, watching Miss Daisy fry that chicken, I couldn't help but think lazily to myself, "How long has it been since you tasted fried chicken?" Now, I never learned how to make fried chicken at the side of my mother, like many young ladies. She wasn't stupid. She always figured I'd make a tremendous mess, then burn out when it came time to clean up. And she was quite right. No, it was my first college roommate, from Firebaugh, California, who taught me the art of making fried chicken. Firebaugh is a town so small that unless you live in Hanford or Lemore, you've probably never heard of it, but it is farm country with a capital "F," where they know how to make fried chicken the way it's supposed to be made! And JoAnn made a fine fried chicken. I simply added beer to the batter and imagined what big pieces of fresh herbs would look and taste like in the breading mix. And if I do say so myself, this is the best fried chicken I've ever tasted!

2 cups flour
½ cup rolled oats
1 teaspoon red
   pepper flakes
¼ cup chopped parsley
Leaves from 6 to 8
   sprigs fresh sage
Leaves from 1 sprig
   fresh rosemary
Leaves from 4 or 5
   sprigs fresh thyme

Leaves from 5 or 6
   sprigs fresh basil
1 tablespoon garlic powder*
1 tablespoon salt
Freshly ground pepper
6 egg whites
1 tablespoon Dijon
   mustard
½ cup beer
Canola oil for frying

---

* If you are wondering why I would use garlic powder in a chapter in which I am adamant about using fresh herbs, I find that fresh garlic burns and turns bitter long before the chicken is done. It's for this reason that, although I am not camping in Antarctica, I recommend using garlic powder.

1. In the workbowl of a food processor, combine flour and oats with all spices and herbs. Process just until herbs are still in discernible pieces (do not powder them). Set aside.

2. Process egg white, mustard, and beer until foamy. Place in a shallow dish.

3. Heat 1 inch of canola oil in a heavy frying pan until medium hot.

4. Dip chicken pieces in egg/beer batter. Then dredge the pieces in the flour mixture.

5. Place floured chicken pieces in hot oil and fry until golden brown on all sides (about 15 to 17 minutes per piece). If your fat is too hot, the chicken will brown before the inside is done. If your fat is too cool, the chicken will soak up a lot of oil. So keep the heat on medium high.

6. Drain and serve as quickly as possible. If you have to refrigerate the chicken, do not cover it. Leaving it uncovered will help to keep it as crisp as possible.

Makes 4 to 6 servings.

Iced Herb Gazpacho

The best gazpacho I ever had was on the highway stretching between Seville and Malaga. And I'm sure part of the reason it tasted so good was that I had been on a plane for 16 hours! I was exhausted, cranky, and finally delighted to find a small inn where I could relax, have a shower, and open my window to find herd of sheep just outside. I crawled down to the restaurant and ordered the only thing that appealed to me—gazpacho. It was a simple pinkish soup with several bowls of stuff to put in it myself: cucumbers, bell peppers, onions, and I can't remember what else. You can choose to put all your ingredients in the gazpacho before you serve it, as suggested here, or you might treat your guests to an herb fest and leave the chopped cucumbers and all the herbs in separate bowls, each labeled, so that they can get a lesson in individual herb flavor components. Either way, it is delicious!

6 large tomatoes	2 scallions, chopped
(peel them if you like)	1 sorrel leaf, deveined
4 cloves fresh garlic,	and coarsely chopped
pressed	Leaves from 2 sprigs
½ cucumber,	fresh basil
peeled and chopped	Leaves from 3 sprigs
¼ teaspoon red	salad burnet
pepper flakes	Leaves from 3 sprigs
¼ cup homemade	cilantro
red wine vinegar	Leaves from 3 sprigs parsley
(see Chapter 4)	Black pepper and
¼ cup olive oil	salt to taste

1. Roughly purée tomatoes, garlic, cucumber, red pepper flakes, vinegar, and oil in the workbowl of the food processor. Leave some texture to the ingredients.

2. Add the herbs and pulse just until chopped. Do not process until smooth or you'll end up with a sort of brown mess. If possible, refrigerate overnight to allow flavors to blend. Serve slightly chilled or at room temperature.

Makes about 4 cups.

Tarragon Potato Salad
with Homemade Garlic Mayonnaise

Everyone, including me, seems to think this potato salad is great. If you do not have a supply of fresh French tarragon (it dies back in winter), you can substitute the heartier Mexican tarragon (*Tagetes lucida*), fresh dill, or cilantro.

4 or 5 large potatoes	⅓ to ½ cup whole fresh
Apple cider or	tarragon leaves, stripped
tarragon vinegar	from their stems
Garlic Mayonnaise	1 red onion or several
(see next recipe)	scallions, chopped
	Salt and pepper to taste

1. Cook and peel the potatoes. Dice them when they are nearly cooled. Douse liberally with apple cider or tarragon vinegar.

2. Add Garlic Mayonnaise to taste, the fresh tarragon, and chopped red onion or scallions. Add salt and pepper to taste. (I rarely use salt in my cooking, but I find that potato salad really needs it.)

3. Mix thoroughly and refrigerate overnight to allow flavors to blend.

Makes 10 servings.

Garlic Mayonnaise

This stuff is deadly. You can vary the garlic content according to taste—6 to 10 cloves make a smashing fresh aioli. Using fresh raw garlic gives the mayo a real "bite."

1 tablespoon white	1 teaspoon Dijon mustard
wine or tarragon	Salt and pepper to taste
vinegar	4 or more cloves garlic
1 large egg*	1½ cups oil

---

* Caution: Due to the overuse of antibiotics and inhumane and unsanitary conditions in the poultry industry, some chickens have developed highly resistant strains of salmonella bacteria that infect even the uncracked eggs. For this reason the U.S. Department of Agriculture has cautioned consumers to avoid eating raw eggs or products made with raw eggs. If you are concerned about salmonella, you may wish to use a commercial brand of mayonnaise for your potato salad.

1. Place vinegar, egg, mustard, salt, pepper, and garlic cloves in the workbowl of a food processor. Mush 'em up.

2. With machine running slowly, drizzle oil in through feed tube. Correct seasonings.

Makes about 2 cups.

Chocolate Peppermint Fudge

Peppermint is really the only mint with enough "guts" to stand up to chocolate. People seem amazed that all the peppermint flavor in this delicious treat comes from peppermint leaves rather than from peppermint extract.

3 cups chocolate chips	1 cup chopped walnuts
1 can (14 oz) sweetened condensed milk	¼ cup finely chopped fresh peppermint
¼ cup (½ stick) butter	leaves (or more)

1. Place chocolate chips, milk, and butter in a bowl and microwave at 50% power for about 5 minutes. (Don't try cooking this at 100% power—the chocolate will burn.)

2. Stir ingredients thoroughly. (Chocolate chips contain a lot of paraffin and will appear not to be melted when they actually are. Just stir them with a fork.) If ingredients are not melted, microwave them at 50% power for another minute or so.

3. Quickly stir in chopped walnuts and chopped peppermint leaves.

4. Spread in a shallow, buttered 9-by-9-inch baking pan and refrigerate until hard (several hours). Or line the pan with aluminum foil and just "pop" the lining and fudge out when hard.

5. Cut into squares and serve.

Makes 12 to 16 squares.

Lemon Verbena Shortbread

Lemon verbena is a shrub native to South America. It is fairly easy to grow (if you don't have a rabbit living in your yard) and will produce a profusion of lemony leaves in the spring and summer. It goes quite bare in the winter. Be sure to use the youngest and most tender leaves and strip out any prominent veins. Pick the leaves just before using, as they dry out very quickly.

1½ cups (3 sticks)
   unsalted butter,
   room temperature
1 cup sugar
3 cups unbleached flour

½ teaspoon salt
⅓ cup fresh lemon
   verbena leaves,
   deveined and chopped

1. Cream the butter and sugar together.
2. Add the flour, salt, and lemon verbena leaves and mix in well.
3. Make a disk out of the dough, wrap it in plastic, and refrigerate it for several hours.
4. Roll out the chilled dough to ½-inch thickness, then cut in some shape that delights you. (I use butterfly or teapot cookie cutters.)
5. Refrigerate your cookies for ½ hour before baking, if possible.
6. Preheat oven to 325°F. Bake cookies for about 30 minutes (or until beginning to brown). Cool on a rack.

Makes about 2 dozen cookies.

Herb Lemonade

This refreshing twist on fresh lemonade can be made with a variety of different herbs, singly or in combination. The most interesting choices are lavender flowers, licorice mint, and rose geranium, while those old standbys, the mints, work beautifully as well. First you make the simple syrup and refrigerate the syrup and herbs overnight so it has a chance to get very strong. Then you make the lemonade using your flavorful herb syrup and adding sprigs of fresh herb to each glass. (You can also keep some simple syrup on hand in the refrigerator for sweetening herb tea. It will keep indefinitely.) This makes enough syrup for three batches of lemonade.

HERB SIMPLE SYRUP:

> 2 cups white sugar
> 2 cups water
>
> 2 cups tightly packed
> fresh herbs

Bring sugar and water to a boil, stirring until sugar is dissolved. Reduce heat and add the fresh herbs. Simmer for about 5 minutes. Cover and allow to cool. (This will help to keep the aromatic oils from escaping.) Steep overnight in the refrigerator. Strain and use as needed.

LEMONADE:

> ⅔ cup freshly squeezed
> lemon juice
> 1 cup herb simple syrup
>
> 4 cups good water
> Several sprigs
> of fresh herbs

Simply mix your ingredients, add ice and a few sprigs of fresh herbs, and serve.

Makes about 6 cups.

CHAPTER 3

Mrs. Caviglia's Surprise, or How to Make Mustard at Home

WHEN I WAS A CHILD, I attended a small parochial school in a town populated by many Irish and Italian Americans. Mrs. Caviglia was the mother of one of our parishioners, and she had been hired to cook a hot lunch for the children each day. I rarely got one. I suspect my mother considered it a frivolous expenditure in a day when pennies counted. But I do remember the "treat" that Mrs. Caviglia handed out to all takers during the morning break. It was an odd treat, to be sure, and I can't imagine where she got the idea, but she expected us all to appreciate it. It was a slice of white bread with nothing but mustard on it, but she handed it out as if it had been spread with the finest grape jelly and thick, creamy peanut butter! Kids who ate in the cafeteria every day had grown used to it and ate greedily. I, for one, thought Mrs. Caviglia was cracked.

Since that time, I have grown to love mustard in all its many manifestations, from good old American "hot dog" mustard to the fancy French Maille and Grey Poupon. Making prepared mustard is a very ancient art. Columella, in his *De Re Rustica* (42 A.D.), gives specific instructions for the making of mustard at home in a mortar and pestle by grinding the seeds and mixing them with water and vinegar. The Romans are credited with being the first to prepare mustard in this manner; they are also credited with distributing its seeds throughout Gaul and Britain. Although I am sure mustard was made in the homes of the "common people" during the Middle Ages (think about it: mustard probably grew wild in many areas of Europe, and it may have been one of the few spices that were free for the taking), it first developed into a bona fide art and commercial venture in the monasteries of the age. Mustard was providing a regular income for the monks of the Abbey of Saint-Germain-des-Près at the time of Charlemagne in 800 A.D. By the fourteenth century, mustard making was the domain of the apothecaries of Dijon. This is only logical, since mustard has been used for centuries as a medication as well as a condiment. (Both Pythagoras and Hippocrates speak highly of its medicinal properties.) Father Junipero Serra brought mustard seed with him to California and, like Hansel and Gretel with their bread crumbs, used it to mark his journey north. To this day, mustard can be seen blossoming its beautiful yellow along the California freeways in the springtime.

When I first became interested in making mustard at home, I held a very fixed notion of what mustard ought to taste like. To me, Grey Poupon was the very apex of mustardom. I thought that if I could create the perfect imitation of Grey Poupon, I'd have achieved success! What I didn't realize is that the beauty and the fun of homemade mustard lies in the fact that you can experiment with textures, flavors, and ingredients to find a blend that suits you to perfection. Made at home in small quantities mustard makes the perfect condiment, as it has done for centuries both in Europe and in Asia.

Mustard seeds can be any one of three types: black mustard seeds (most commonly used for all commercially prepared European mustards before World War II and the most pungent of the mustards), brown mustard seeds (now most commonly used for all commercial European mustards because of its greater ease in mechanical harvesting), and the milder white or yellow mustard (the main ingredient in "hot dog" mustard). Brown and yellow seeds are used almost exclusively in the commercial industry, since black mustard can be harvested only by hand (the seeds are smaller than brown or yellow seeds). Brown or yellow seeds can easily be obtained through mail order or at specialty food and spice stores, while black mustard seeds are most easily obtained from Indian markets (whole black mustard seeds being a common ingredient in Indian cooking). For the home mustard maker, brown or yellow seeds ought to be sufficient to produce a good mustard.

The lion's share of the world's mustard seeds are grown in the "prairie" provinces and states of the United States and Canada, on land suitable for growing wheat. They are harvested by grain-processing equipment, using techniques perfected in the cereal industry! The quality of mustard seed (just like that of any agricultural product) will vary according to the season and the geographical location in which it is grown. Government grading standards for mustard seeds, based upon the percentage of damaged, heated, or green seeds and unavoidable adulteration with other types of seeds, are applied to the mustard seed crop of both Canada (the world's largest producer of mustard seed) and the United States. "No. 1 Canada" designates the top of the line in the minds of most experts.

Mustard can be prepared in a variety of textures. Mustard powder mixed with a liquid will produce a very smooth, but also very hot mustard (the "heat" is contained in the endosperm, the "meat" of the seeds, not the hull). Japanese mustard is traditionally a simple mixture of mustard powder and water blended together shortly before serving. Coleman's mustard powder has gained enormous popularity in England, where it, too, is simply mixed with water shortly before being served with the evening meal. (To "cut" the heat, flour is added to any mustard powder sold in England.) Dry mustard powder, a common ingredient in oil-and-vinegar salad dressings, is used not only for its flavor contribution, but because it acts as an emulsifying agent. A mixture of mustard powder with some coarsely ground mustard seed will produce a coarsely grained, country-style mustard. And a very coarse mustard can be made by using only coarsely ground mustard seeds.

As with many other herbs and spices, what makes mustard flavorful and hot is largely, in brown mustard, its essential oil content. The predominant flavoring agent in yellow mustard is a similar but nonvolatile sulfur compound. Mixing mustard with cold water or liquids develops these flavor compounds, intensifying their flavor and pungency. Using hot water or applying heat to the mustard will dissipate the intensity somewhat (making a milder mustard) but will also tend to dissipate the more delicate nuances of flavor (as it will with any herb or spice). Commercial mustard companies are careful, in both the milling and preparing of mustards, not to raise the temperature above 110°F so as to preserve the flavor components. Although numerous recipes call for cooking or heating your mustard while making it, this is not done by the mustard purist. If you intend to use your prepared mustard as an ingredient in a recipe, you may want to keep this in mind and add it during the last few minutes of cooking.

Grinding Mustard Seed

To grind mustard seeds at home for your own mustard, you can break them up with a mortar and pestle, or you can process them in an electric coffee mill. (I keep one electric coffee grinder that is used exclusively for spice grinding, since the oily residues may give an "off" flavor to your coffee.) There is no correct texture or degree to which you can or should grind your seeds; there is only the texture that suits you best! Process as little or as long, as smooth or as fine as you like.

Purchasing Mustard Seed

It is best to purchase your mustard seeds from a supplier with a rapid turnover. An Indian food market, a grocery store that does a good, brisk business in spices, or a reliable mail order supplier (such as the ones listed at the back of this book) are usually excellent sources. While testing recipes, I purchased some dry mustard and some mustard seed from my local grocery store. They were nationally known name-brand spices and seemed fairly fresh and flavorful. (The name-brand mustard seeds and powders you purchase in the spice section of your grocery store will more than likely be the yellow variety. Brown seeds seem to be more of a specialty item and too hot for the average American consumer.)

Additions to Mustard

Additions to mustard can be many. The Mount Horeb Mustard Museum in Mount Horeb, Wisconsin, counts more than 1700 types of prepared mustard in its collection. Additives include honey, garlic, horseradish, fresh herbs of all types, citrus, peppercorns, spices, nettle leaves, shallots, peanuts, olives, seeds, fruits, chilies, and cider, to name just a few! Although such adulterated concoctions may hold some popular appeal, I personally prefer my mustard to taste precisely like what it is: mustard. I like it fairly simple.

Keep in mind that any mustard you make at home is likely to be a bit more runny and considerably more pungent than commercially prepared mustards. Homemade mustards may also taste almost unpleasant when first made up, but if you allow their flavor to develop for at least 24 hours, you should taste some remarkable and pleasant changes. Remember that using brown powder and seed will yield a more pungent end product than will yellow powder and seed.

The Mustard Lab

Part of the pleasure of making mustard at home is that you can vary the textures and flavors to suit the occasion and your personal taste. To familiarize yourself with some of the common variations on a theme, you could try the following experiments.

EXPERIMENTING WITH LIQUID INGREDIENTS

Mustard has been mixed with many different types of liquids since the days of the ancient Romans, who mixed it with wine. To experience the effect that different liquids have upon mustard, make a few little piles (1 tablespoon each) of mustard powder. Mix a different kind of liquid into each pile. Try water, sherry vinegar, white wine vinegar, red wine vinegar, champagne, wine, sherry, stout malt liquor or malt vinegar, and plain grape juice for openers. For a more interesting punch, try using various liqueurs with your powder. Taste your concoctions. Some of them may be downright unpleasant. Allow them to develop for an hour or two and then taste them again.

EXPERIMENTING WITH SEEDS

You might like to see if you can tell any difference between brown mustard powder and yellow mustard powder. Purchase some of each and make a little pile (1 tablespoon) of each, then add water and mix. Are there flavor differences? Are there differences in aroma? (There definitely should be!)

Try tasting whole mustard seeds: brown, black, and yellow. Can you taste the differences among them? (This is how the Egyptians, Indians, and Chinese seemed to use mustard seeds in ancient times—they simply ate them whole.)

Then try experimenting with texture. First make a smooth paste, using only mustard powder and water. (This is how the English have used Coleman's mustard for some years. Just powder and water and roast beef!) Then try making a coarser country-style mustard. Blend half mustard powder and half coarsely ground mustard seeds with water. For a very earthy, coarse mustard, use nothing but coarsely ground seeds. (You can grind seeds fairly fine using a coffee mill, or you can grind them coarsely in either a coffee mill or a mortar and pestle.) I prefer to vary the texture according to the occasion and food being served. Sometimes I prefer a more refined, smooth mustard (usually sweet) and sometimes, for a more "rustic" effect or dish, I prefer a grainy mustard. After you have familiarized yourself with the basic components of prepared mustard, you can then experiment in your mustard lab to find a combination which suits your own needs.

Some Mustard Recipes

The following are two of my favorite, very basic recipes for making good mustard at home, with an added "fancy" mustard thrown in for good measure.

Basic Country-Style Mustard

This recipe yields about ⅔ cup of pungent, grainy, all-purpose mustard. This, to me, is "real" mustard. From it, all else springs!

2 tablespoons coarsely ground brown mustard seeds	¼ cup brown or yellow mustard powder
2 tablespoons coarsely ground yellow mustard seeds	¼ cup cold water
	2 tablespoons vinegar (white wine or apple cider)
	1 teaspoon salt

1. Grind your mustard seeds to the texture you desire. (Remember, there is no correct texture.)

2. Mix the mustard powder, ground seeds, and water together. Allow the mixture to stand for about 10 minutes.

3. Add the vinegar and salt and blend. For best results, store in the refrigerator overnight before serving.

Makes about 1 cup.

Hot and Sweet Mustard

Mustard has been mixed with a variety of liquids through the centuries: the juice of unripe grapes (verjuice), must (freshly crushed grapes and their skins), beer or ale, water, red wine, champagne, and various vinegars, to name a few. Each produces a unique result. This particular mustard needs at least 24 hours for its full "mustard" flavor to develop.

½ cup yellow
  or brown mustard
  powder
¼ cup orange
  flavored liqueur

3 tablespoons sherry
  or white wine vinegar
¼ cup dark brown sugar
1 teaspoon salt

Mix all ingredients together into a smooth paste. Allow the blend to stand for at least 24 hours before using.

Makes about 1 cup.

Grainy Apricot Mustard

The thought of apricot preserves mixed with mustard may not appeal to you at first, but a fruit and mustard combination is nothing new. The Italian *mostarda di cremona* is a blend consisting predominantly of fruit and mustard.

¼ cup good apricot
   preserves
¼ cup yellow or
   brown mustard powder
2 tablespoons each
   yellow and brown
   mustard seeds,
   coarsely ground

3 tablespoons
   white wine vinegar
1 tablespoon
   good balsamic vinegar
1 teaspoon salt

Blend all ingredients together and allow the mustard to stand for at least 24 hours before serving.

Makes about ¾ cup.

A Mustard Menu

Grainy Mustard Soufflé

❧

Green Salad with Bacon,
Sun-Dried Tomatoes and
Hot and Sweet Mustard Vinaigrette

❧

Grilled Chicken with
Apricot Mustard, Fennel Seed,
and Peppercorn Marinade

❧

Cheddar Chive Biscuits (recipe in Chapter 6)
with Grainy Mustard Butter
(recipe in Chapter 7)

❧

Summer Fruits with
Fresh Goat's Milk Ricotta and
Apricot Vinegar with Brown Mustard Seeds

❧

Suggested Wines: French White Burgundy
or California Chardonnay

The tangy bite of mustard forms an excellent counterpoint to all sorts of flavors and foods, and it is used in cultures and cuisines throughout the world, from Asia to the New World. This menu offers a sampler of ingredients with which mustard has an affinity.

Grainy Mustard Soufflé

The full flavor and grainy texture of the Basic Country-Style Mustard lend an interesting dimension to that old favorite, the cheese soufflé. The tiny grains of mustard sort of pop in your mouth!

2½ tablespoons butter	5 egg whites
3 tablespoons flour	½ cup grated sharp
1 cup milk, heated	Cheddar cheese
3 or 4 tablespoons	½ cup grated
Basic Country-Style	Gruyère cheese
Mustard	3 tablespoons coarsely
4 egg yolks	chopped fresh tarragon

1. Preheat the oven to 400°F.

2. Prepare a soufflé dish with a collar made of aluminum foil, parchment, or waxed paper. Butter both the dish and the collar.

3. Melt the butter and flour together. Cook this roux for a minute or two.

4. Add hot milk and stir over medium-high heat until sauce thickens.

5. Remove from heat and stir in mustard and egg yolks, one at a time.

6. Beat egg whites until stiff but not dry.

7. Incorporate 3 or 4 tablespoons of the mustard mixture into egg whites.

8. Gently fold the remaining mustard mixture into the egg whites, a bit at a time, adding sprinkles of cheese and chopped tarragon.

9. Pour mixture carefully into prepared soufflé dish. Turn oven down to 375°F and bake soufflé for 35 to 40 minutes without opening the oven door.

10. Remove from oven and serve immediately, as the soufflé will deflate rapidly.

Makes 4 servings.

Green Salad with Red Potato, Bacon, Sun-Dried Tomatoes, and Hot and Sweet Mustard Vinaigrette

Perhaps the best greens you could use for this salad would be a combination of arugula and young, tender mustard greens. Both stand up well to the potent mustard vinaigrette.

6 cups mixed arugula and young mustard greens

6 red potatoes, steamed just until tender and sliced

3 or 4 strips bacon, cooked until crisp, well-drained and crumbled

2 tablespoons sun-dried tomatoes, sliced into strips*

3 to 4 tablespoons Hot and Sweet Mustard Vinaigrette

Mix all ingredients together in a salad bowl, cover with Hot and Sweet Mustard Vinaigrette, and toss gently but thoroughly. (You may wish to add the potato slices last to avoid breaking them.)

Makes 4 servings.

---

* Until recently, nearly all sun-dried tomatoes were available packed in oil. I dry tomatoes from my own garden in the oven for 24 hours at 250°F, then simply store them in the freezer, in an effort to cut down on calories.

Hot and Sweet Mustard Vinaigrette

This piquant vinaigrette is the perfect dressing for a salad of leafy greens with diced red potatoes, chopped sun-dried tomatoes, and crumbled bacon. (It's also great over a platter of green beans.)

¼ cup good vegetable oil   1 tablespoon sherry vinegar
¼ cup Hot and Sweet   1 teaspoon grated fresh
   Mustard   ginger root

Whisk all ingredients together briskly until somewhat emulsified. Allow flavors to blend overnight before serving.

Makes about ½ cup.

Apricot Mustard, Fennel Seed, and Peppercorn Marinade

This flavorful marinade is good on grilled poultry or pork. Make the marinade up at least 24 hours ahead of time so that the flavors in it have a chance to blend.

½ tablespoon fresh   ½ cup Grainy Apricot
   black peppercorns,   Mustard (see page 67)
   crushed   ½ cup oil
1 tablespoon fennel seed   1 cup apricot preserves
¼ cup stout ale   6 cloves garlic, chopped
¼ cup apple cider   2 whole chicken breasts,
   vinegar or lemon juice   or 4 breast halves

1. Crack the peppercorns coarsely in a mortar and pestle or a spice mill. Add the fennel seeds and crack slightly.

2. Blend ale, vinegar, mustard, oil, apricot preserves, and garlic in a blender until emulsified.

3. Add cracked peppercorns and fennel seed and mix in.

4. Allow flavors to blend for at least 24 hours, then marinate chicken for 24 hours in the marinade.

5. Grill over medium-hot coals.

Makes 4 servings.

Summer Fruits with Fresh Goat's Milk Ricotta and Apricot Vinegar with Brown Mustard Seeds

Choose a mélange of your favorite summer fruits (cherries, kiwi, and peaches, for instance) and arrange them, sliced if necessary, attractively on individual plates. Top each portion with three scoops of freshly made goat's milk ricotta cheese (see Chapter 5), using a small oval ice cream scoop available at gourmet cookware shops. Drizzle each salad with a very sweet version of Apricot Vinegar with Brown Mustard Seeds (see Chapter 4).

CHAPTER 4

Sour Grapes, or How to Make Good Vinegar at Home

SEVERAL YEARS AGO, while vacationing in Paris, I went in search of the well-known confectionery, Fouquet, where, it was touted (by my Gault-Millau guide), Mme. Fouquet made an impressive array of flavored vinegars in her "15th arrondissement laboratory." With all the many pleasant distractions Paris has to offer, I never did find Fouquet and the aforementioned vinegars, but I did come home with a burning curiosity about just how one sets about making vinegar! A search of the existing literature revealed very little of use to the aspiring home vinegar maker, so my search was mostly a process of gathering bits of information whenever and wherever I could. George and Piret Munger, local restaurateurs and "foodies," helped me locate my first "mother"; it had been brought to the United States ten years earlier by a Swiss woman living in La Jolla. (I remember how fascinated I was to see the slimy mass of cellulose growing in the two ceramic crocks she had in her kitchen.) I carefully carried my new "mother" home and began a jar of my own, a jar that eventually blossomed into jugs—huge two-gallon olive jugs—and an assortment of mason jars, bowls, and oak barrels. I discovered for myself that the best vinegar is that which you make at home in your own kitchen! The process is fairly simple, and there are few things that can go wrong. You can't poison yourself or your family (too much alcohol and acid) and you will end up with a vinegar that is stronger, more robust, and more flavorful than anything you have ever tasted before.

Bacteria Turn Wine into Vinegar

The first detailed description of vinegar production was made by the famous French gardener and landscape artist Olivier de Serres in 1616, but it remained for Louis Pasteur, more than two hundred years later, to identify the cause of the conversion! In a country whose national economy depended so heavily on the export and sale of wine, Pasteur's fame and popularity revolved around his discoveries related to wine spoilage more than anything else.

It was Pasteur who discovered that not only were bacteria responsible for the conversion of alcohol into acetic acid, but that those bacteria required the presence of oxygen in order to function. He demonstrated that wine sealed in a bottle without air would remain stable for an indeterminate length of time and that, conversely, wine left exposed to air would inevitably turn to vinegar. Part of Pasteur's remedy for the problem rested in the technique that came to be known as pasteurization, which killed any bacteria present in the wine without significantly altering its flavor. And part of the solution lay in sealing wine bottles to make them airtight.

Winemakers of today have even more sophisticated and effective methods of rendering their wines unspoilable, most notably that of adding the smallest amount of sulfur dioxide to the finished product to kill any bacteria that may be present. This is good news for the winemaker—it stabilizes and thus extends the shelf life of his product. But its presence is an annoyance to the would-be home vinegar maker because it kills the very bacteria (called acetobacter) responsible for turning alcohol into acetic acid. In my mother's day, every Italian family in the neighborhood had a bottle of uncorked Chianti sitting in the cellar turning to vinegar all of its own accord. Today, thanks to modern technology, the vinegar enthusiast must resort to more sophisticated means of introducing the appropriate bacteria to his or her wine bottle.

How to Get Your Vinegar Started

There are two fairly reliable methods of starting a vinegar. One is to find a gourmet cook in your area who already has a healthy supply of vinegar going, with several layers of that mysterious substance known as the "mother" growing in it. A vinegar mother looks a lot like a wet, pliable piece of shoe leather—smooth, rubbery, and burgundy (or grey, if your "mother" forms in white wine) in color. It is composed primarily of cellulose and bacteria and will eventually form on the surface of any wine that contains a lively colony of acetobacter. At first, you may think your wine is developing patches of mold on its surface. *Not so.* The patches will expand to cover the entire surface of the wine and will begin to form the gelatinous mass known as the mother. After one layer forms, it often drops to the bottom of your container and a new layer forms on the surface. Periodically, you need to remove layers of mother and either give them the heave-ho or use them to begin new jars of vinegar.

Another method of starting your vinegar barrel is to use a good unpasteurized vinegar. The vinegar you make yourself is un pasteurized vinegar, and it contains live bacterial cultures that will turn wine into vinegar. Unpasteurized vinegar can be purchased at health food stores or through wine supply shops. (See "Sources" at the end of this book.) If it is truly unpasteurized and still contains a living bacterial culture, you can simply add it to your wine and wait. The problem I have found is that not all commercial unpasteurized vinegar is viable. Purchase from a reliable wine supply merchant to ensure best results.

CHOOSING YOUR WINE STOCK

Your wine stock is simply the wine from which your vinegar is made. Starting with a flavorful wine or beer means your finished product will be flavorful and interesting. Conversely, a weak or insipid wine will produce a fairly mundane vinegar. The most simple and traditional of methods is to empty all leftover bottles of wine into the vinegar barrel. Then empty all leftover glasses of wine into the vinegar barrel. That's right, don't be squeamish. Why waste good wine? You have to remember that one of the reasons both wine and vinegar have been companions to humans for so long is that either the alcohol content or the acid content is so high that no organisms harmful to people can live in them! Organisms may make a wine taste lousy, but they can't make you sick.

If you are more of a purist, you may choose to purchase bottles of one particular varietal for your barrel. I have often made decent vinegar from gallons of jug red wine, and I currently purchase cabernet sauvignon straight from the barrel of one of the best winemakers in our local Temecula Valley. The resultant vinegar is rustic and vigorous. I have often fantasized about setting up barrels of barbera and zinfandel to taste-test!

White wines may take a bit more skill to culture, and there are a number of reasons why. Probably the most significant is that both the color and flavor of white wines tend to be more fragile than that of the reds, so there is a tendency for winemakers to sulfite them a bit more heavily. Too great a concentration of sulfites can kill any acetobacter culture you might add. A good idea is to dilute your white wines by one-third with good water, just to make sure the solution is one in which the acetobacter can live. I generally find that hearty chardonnay and champagne stock make the best white vinegars. Other varieties just don't seem to have enough flavor components to make interesting vinegars.

Vinegar can, of course, be made from sherry (sherry vinegar) or beer (malt vinegar) or any beverage with an alcohol content of around 10 to 12 percent. I have even tried Diana Kennedy's recipe for making a mild pineapple vinegar from scratch with good results. (From Ms. Kennedy's book *The Cuisines of Mexico*, to make a mild vinegar called for in some Mexican recipes, you add the peel of half a pineapple, ¼ cup dark brown sugar, and a small segment of pineapple flesh to 1 quart of water. Cover tightly and set the jar in a sunny or warm spot. In a few days the mixture will begin to ferment, then change color and become more acid. In 2 to 3 weeks, the process of acetification should have been completed. It works and is an amusing experiment in watching the whole process of vinegar making from beginning to end. Just watch out for fruit flies and don't expect a hearty end product!)

CHOOSING AN APPROPRIATE CONTAINER

After you have chosen a suitable stock for your vinegar making, you need to choose an appropriate container in which to make it. Easiest of all is to take an empty, very clean gallon jug, fill it half full of wine (the acetobacter need plenty of oxygen in which to do their work), add your bacterial culture and cover the jug with cheesecloth, securing it with a rubber band. Leave the jug undisturbed in a warm, fairly dark place until it smells and tastes more like vinegar than wine; then bottle it! (This may take anywhere from three to six months, depending on the weather, the type of wine you use, and the strength of the initial bacterial culture.)

For a touch of class, you may wish to make your vinegar in an oak barrel. A small barrel (one or two gallons) makes an attractive rustic addition to the kitchen or dining area and should easily keep your family in great vinegar the year around. Barrels tend to be expensive (small barrels run around $80) because there is only one reliable producer of small barrels in the United States, but they last a lifetime and impart a wonderful oaky flavor and aroma to the finished product. (See "Sources" at the end of this book.) If you do not wish to invest in a barrel right away, you can purchase oak chips from a wine supply merchant and add them to your glass gallon jug just for a hint of oak. As a French friend of mine remarked simply when he tasted some of my barrel vinegar, "Mama!" because his mother, like all good Provençal *mamans*, always kept a small barrel of vinegar going in the kitchen.

To set a small barrel up for vinegar production, you need to enlarge the already extant bunghole to ensure proper aeration and allow removal of any buildup of mother that may accrue. (I generally enlarge the hole to a diameter of 2½ to 3 inches, a size through which I can fit my hand.) You will also need to purchase a small spigot and tap it into the bottom of one end of the barrel. You may also want to drill a small hole near the top of each end of the barrel to get some cross-ventilation. Once you have properly prepared your barrel, fill it with water and allow it to soak for a day or two. All barrels leak at first, but the wood swells as it absorbs liquid, making it watertight. This process may take a day or two. At the end of two days, empty out the water, replace it with your chosen wine, and add your vinegar culture. Be sure to cover all holes tightly with a fine grade of cheesecloth, or you may be inundated with fruit flies! I actually glue my cheesecloth lightly to the barrel.

Assessing the Finished Product

Your nose is the best tool you have for assessing when the vinegar is done. Smell the stuff. If it smells more like vinegar than wine, if it "bites" your nose, it's done. Taste it. If it really makes your mouth pucker, it's done. (Occasionally vinegar may develop some "off" odors, the most common being that of ethyl acetate, the familiar smell of fingernail polish remover. Before you throw your vinegar out, try aerating it. Pour your vinegar back and forth from one jug to another several times. Then let it rest for a day or two. Incorporating oxygen into the brew will usually dissipate any "off" odors that may develop.) Several male students of mine have clev-

erly suggested adding either a fish tank aerator to the vinegar barrel, or a type of aerator used to keep live fishing bait alive when
you go fishing. I haven't tried either method, but both sound in-
triguing and workable.

When your vinegar clearly tastes and smells like vinegar to
you, it's time to bottle it. Don't leave it sitting around for an indeterminate period of time. The same acetobacter which initially
converted the alcohol in the wine to acetic acid can also go on to
convert acetic acid to carbon dioxide and water. So it's important
to neutralize the action of the bacteria once the process of acetification is complete. To do this, either you need to kill all bacteria
present in the vinegar by pasteurizing it (raise the temperature to
150°F, then cap it quickly before it cools), or you need to cut off
its oxygen supply by filling your bottles as full as possible, then
capping them tightly.

Bottling and Sealing the Finished Product

Now that the vinegar is complete, it's time to bottle it. Many
attractive bottles for vinegar are available in gourmet shops
throughout the country. I use a simple green glass 375-milliliter
Bordeaux-type bottle and cork from my local wine supply store.
Make sure your bottles are thoroughly clean and free of any soapy
residue. Strain the vinegar through fine-grade cheesecloth into the
very clean bottles. (There are more sophisticated methods of fin-
ing, or clarifying, the vinegar if you feel you want a clearer product, and any good wine supply store should be able to provide you
with equipment and instructions on these methods. I'm happy
with the rustic and somewhat cloudy appearance of my freshly
made "cabs.") Fill the bottle as full as possible (we now wish to exclude oxygen from the vinegar). Then cap it tightly with a new cork.

For an added touch of class, I cut a 4-inch strip of colored
grosgrain ribbon and drape it across the top of the cap. I then fill
an empty orange juice can with household paraffin and set it in a

pan of hot water to melt. (Do not heat paraffin directly over a flame if you value your eyebrows and forelocks!) When the paraffin has melted, turn the bottle upside down and dip its top into the melted paraffin, while holding onto the ribbon. Do this several times until a nice paraffin seal has formed. I have my own personalized gold-stamped labels that I then put on the bottles. For special occasions and gift giving, I form a small herb wreath for the neck of the bottle, using medium-gauge florist's wire and a prostrate variety of rosemary, oregano, or marjoram. Small herb flowers that dry well, such as yellow santolina blossoms or yarrow, can be added for color.

Aging Your Vinegar

Good vinegar, like good wine, improves with aging. Young, freshly made vinegar often has a sharp "bite" to it that will curl your hair; it mellows after six months or so in the bottle, stored under the same steady, cool temperatures you would use for a good wine. Just remember to store your bottles away from light and extremes of heat or cold.

Using Your Vinegar

Your finished vinegar, whether white or red, will be stronger and more flavorful than anything you can buy, so you will want to use it sparingly. I find that an herb red wine vinegar makes an excellent dressing (together with my favorite fruity California olive oil) for robust salad greens and garden vegetables, as well as an excellent base for marinades. White wine and champagne vinegars can be used for slightly more delicate jobs.

Some Vinegar Recipes

Good Raspberry Vinegar

Fruit vinegars are traditionally made by adding fruit and sugar to vinegar, allowing them to macerate (soak) for a week or two, then straining. A good, fresh raspberry vinegar can be delicious. (My friend Bonnie made some of the best I have ever tasted one year, using raspberries from her own garden.) But here is a recipe for a brilliantly colorful, intensely flavorful raspberry vinegar that is·so thick you can use it by itself as a salad dressing. As with nut oils, the enemy is oxygen. Oxygen tends to turn fruit brown and accelerate the decay process, so you want to keep any leftover vinegar in small bottles, tightly capped, in the refrigerator.

> 2 cups fresh (or frozen)
> raspberries
> 2 tablespoons sugar
> (this may vary according
> to personal taste)
>
> 2 cups white wine
> vinegar or champagne
> vinegar

1. Gently heat the raspberries and sugar for a minute or two. Stir and cool.

2. Place the vinegar, berries, and sugar in a blender and purée until smooth. Store in a small, airtight bottle in the refrigerator until ready to use. (This will give you a very thick, brightly colored vinegar. For a bit less texture, strain through a fine-mesh sieve.)

Makes about 3 cups.

Apricot Vinegar
with Brown Mustard Seeds

Good apricot vinegar can be made with either fresh or dried, sulfured apricots. Using fresh apricots produces a spectacular vinegar and you can do so by following the simple instructions in the previous recipe for making raspberry vinegar, since that technique works for nearly all fresh fruits. If you'd like to make your vinegar from dried fruit, I suggest using sulfured apricots because the sulfur is used to retain their pretty, bright orange color. (Unsulfured apricots taste great but are an unappetizing brown color.) You may wish to inform guests that there are sulfites (a minimal pinch) in this vinegar, on the off chance that someone is allergic to them. Make this vinegar nice and sweet, and use it to finish the Summer Fruits with Fresh Goat's Milk Ricotta in Chapter 3.

½ cup dried apricots
  (or more if you
  want a thicker vinegar)
2 cups white wine
  vinegar or champagne
  vinegar

2 tablespoons sugar
  (or more to taste)
1 or 2 tablespoons whole
  brown mustard seeds

1. Soak the apricots in some of the vinegar overnight to soften them.

2. Place a cup of vinegar in the blender with the undrained apricots and sugar and blend until fairly smooth.

3. Add the rest of the vinegar, a little at a time, until you reach a nice, thick texture. You may not need to add all the vinegar.

4. Mix in mustard seeds, and store vinegar in the refrigerator until needed.

Makes about 2 cups.

The Gilded Lily:
Making Herb Vinegar

Initially I felt that my vinegars were so good that adding herbs would simply be a case of gilding the lily, but after a few experiments, I decided a gilded lily was even better than an ungilded lily. I don't usually flavor white wine vinegars with herbs; I either serve them by themselves or reserve them for fruit vinegar, such as the Raspberry Vinegar recipe given here. The reds, however, tend to be heartier and more complex, and they stand up well to a myriad of resinous, earthy mountain herbs. Pack a wide-mouthed gallon jug (the manager of the local supermarket deli saves them for me) with herb cuttings. Pack them in fairly tightly; make sure the jar is full of herbs. Rosemary, oregano, savory, sage, thyme, marjoram, bay, hyssop, basil, cat thyme, and garlic alternately grace my hearty red wine vinegars. Pour your home-made wine vinegar into the jar, on top of the herbs; cover the whole thing tightly with cheesecloth, and allow the herbs to macerate in the vinegar until it smells and tastes the way you want it to smell and taste. (This may take anywhere from one to four weeks, depending on how strong an herb flavor you want to impart to the vinegar.) Strain the finished herb vinegar and pack it into tightly sealed bottles as per the instructions given earlier. This is very strong stuff (but very exciting) and should be used sparingly!

An Assortment of Salads

Green Salad Dressed with
Oil and Vinegar

I remember the first time I realized that making a green salad was an art. I was taking a cooking class from Michel Stroot, the very talented chef at The Golden Door, an exclusive spa in San Diego County. One of the things he made was a simple green salad, and I was amazed to see that he dressed an enormous bowl full of greens with a minuscule amount of vinaigrette. The secret, he explained, was simply to toss the greens carefully and thoroughly, and if you did that, you would find that a small amount of dressing would go a very long way.

To make a really good green salad, I would recommend that you grow your own greens. To do so means that you can enjoy a wide variety of greens (and for that matter, reds) that might not ordinarily be available to you in the supermarket. And you will be able to enjoy them just hours after they are picked. (I say hours because I always refrigerate my garden greens for an hour or two before serving.) Perusing specialty vegetable catalogs (such as Shepherd's Garden Seeds and Seeds Blum listed under "Sources" at the end of this book) is a terrific way to pass the rainy days of winter.

After you have picked your greens (or, OK, bought them at the supermarket), be sure to wash them thoroughly. No one likes to find unexpected protein in their salads or pick grit from between their teeth. And secondly, *dry them thoroughly*. This is a cardinal rule, because oil and water don't mix. If you put an oil based dressing on leaves that are coated with water, it won't stick, and you can guess where most of your carefully made dressing will end up!

After you have dried your greens thoroughly, chill them for a bit in the refrigerator. This cold treatment will crisp and refresh the greens. And then, at the last moment, just before serving, dress your salad with your own homemade herb and garlic vinegar (see "The Gilded Lily") and just a small amount of olive oil. Toss thoroughly. You can always add more oil or vinegar, but you cannot easily resurrect a "runny" salad or one with an overdose of vinegar. Sprinkle lightly with salt if you think it is needed, then grind a bit of fresh pepper over it.

Apple Walnut Salad with Persimmon Vinegar

The classic Waldorf Salad was first served at New York's Waldorf Hotel in the late 19th century. This is a variation on that theme, using persimmon vinegar and walnut oil in place of the usual mayonnaise. I recommend you use tart Granny Smith apples or, better yet, if you grow your own, a variety of fresh-picked apples from your own trees! I'm of the opinion that the guy who named Golden Delicious apples was drunk at the time. The persimmon vinegar should be so thick you can omit the oil and never miss it.

4 large Granny Smith apples	Persimmon vinegar (follow instructions for Raspberry Vinegar)
1 cup chopped celery	
1 cup shelled walnuts, lightly toasted	Walnut oil (follow instructions for Hazelnut Oil in Chapter 7)
1 head lettuce	Freshly ground cinnamon

1. Wash your apples thoroughly and cut them in cubes of a suitable size (about 1-inch).

2. Toss apples, celery, and lightly toasted walnuts together and mound on a bed of lettuce.

3. Drizzle first with persimmon vinegar to taste, then with walnut oil. (Drizzling the oils on separately and last makes a more attractive and colorful presentation than mixing them all together would.)

4. Sprinkle with coarse freshly ground cinnamon.

Makes 6 servings.

Tandoori Chicken Salad
with Kiwi Vinegar

Curried anything tastes good to me. I especially like pairing chicken that has marinated in a relatively hot curry marinade with the cooling, tart flavor and bright green color of the kiwi vinegar.

4 chicken breast halves	¼ cup fresh cilantro leaves
4 cups fresh greens	2 scallions, thinly sliced
Kiwi vinegar (follow	4 teaspoons sesame seeds,
instructions for	lightly toasted
Raspberry Vinegar)	

1. Marinate the chicken breasts in Curry Marinade (recipe follows) overnight, then grill over medium-hot coals.

2. Place 1 cup of greens on each of 4 plates.

3. Slice the cooling chicken breasts and place each on a bed of lettuce. Drizzle Kiwi Vinegar over the sliced chicken.

4. Sprinkle each salad with 1 tablespoon fresh cilantro, 1 teaspoon sliced scallions, and 1 teaspoon sesame seeds.

Makes 4 servings.

Curry Marinade

1 cup vegetable oil	2 teaspoons honey
2 tablespoons	2 or 3 cloves garlic
curry powder	1 teaspoon salt
1 tablespoon Tahini	

Place all ingredients in a blender and whir until smooth.

CHAPTER 5

The Poor Man's Cow, or How to Make Goat Cheese Chez Vous

ONE OF MY FIRST MEMORIES of goats came second-hand. I remember rainy winter evenings by the fire when my mother first read to me from Johanna Spyri's *Heidi*. Heidi's grandfather, whom she dearly loved, owned two goats. I remember the vivid mental images I formed of green mountain pastures dotted with edelweiss, of the small cottage in which Heidi and her grandfather lived, of their simple morning meal of a bowl of goat's milk. (What a strange breakfast that seemed! My grandfather and I ate bacon, eggs, and mountains of fried potatoes!) But beneath it all, I remember the feeling that these were, for her, the happiest years of all.

Only when I was much older did I make the acquaintance of my first real-life goat, and I have to admit I was utterly charmed by her funny little goat face, her delicate cloven hooves, and her friendly, puppy-dog-like demeanor.

And only when I was older still (on my first trip to France) did I discover that I had been missing one of life's great culinary joys, goat cheese! I would buy bags of *crottins* and Montrachet to bring home, coerce the Air France stews into stowing my loot in some corner of the refrigerator, and arrive home to weeks of salads, omelets, toasts, and plain nibbles of hard goat cheese. Imagine my delight when Laura Chenel first began producing goat cheese in California.

The goat is most commonly known as the poor man's cow, and has been a companion to humans for centuries. (The goat was the first of the ruminants to be domesticated, in about the seventh century B.C.) More economical than the cow because of her smaller size; tough enough to survive in terrain that is either too hot, too dry, or too steep for the cow; undiscriminating about her food supply (the lining of the goat's mouth and digestive tract enable her to digest brambles, thistles, and twigs); very sociable and a relatively bright animal to boot, the goat has provided humans with milk on the hoof for centuries. The Roman poet Catullus wrote:

> The dainty she-goat from my pastures
> Bears to the city her teats distended with milk.

The portable nature of the goat's bounty made her a not uncommon passenger aboard ship before the days of refrigeration. She was a constant and sure source of milk for the sailors and could be left on an island to ensure milk for future passersby. (St. Helena Island, to which Napoleon was exiled, had been almost completely deforested by the goats left behind by its Portuguese discoverers.)

Goat's milk has generally been safer than that of the cow. TB and brucellosis were far less prevalent in goats than in cows, and the bacterial count of the dairy goat's milk was and is still generally lower than that of cow's milk. Goat's milk has become a popular substitute for cow's milk among infants and the lactose intolerant. It contains less lactose than cow's milk and its fat globules are smaller and more easily digestible. The pure white color of goat's milk is owing to the fact that all its beta carotene has been converted to vitamin A.

Aside from offering a sanitary and economical alternative to the cow, the goat possesses a naturally calm, friendly disposition which makes her a good companion to humans. (A horse in the face of danger will panic and run; a goat will stand her ground, face danger, and rely upon her agility to outmaneuver an attacker. During World War I, goats were sometimes used to shepherd horses out of areas of explosives or gunfire; left on their own, the horses would have become unmanageably panic stricken.) The expression "to get your goat" comes from the horse-racing circuit, where companion goats have been used to calm the naturally temperamental racehorse. If you wanted to affect the outcome of a race, you would steal the top competitor's companion goat before a big race, thus throwing the champ into a stew!

Goats today are most prevalent in developing nations. India, Africa, and the countries of Latin America all rely upon the goat to supply their people with both milk and meat. Greece and Spain lead the European pack, and France is the world's leading producer of goat cheeses. While goat's milk and cheeses have been a part of the peasant diet around the world for centuries, only in the last ten years have affluent Americans (and, wouldn't you know it, Californians) turned their attention to its charms. First was Laura Chenel, who left Sonoma County for France to learn the trade in 1979, then came a slew of others, all catering to the growing yuppie hunger for chèvre!

Making Simple Cheeses

Making cheese ought to be a fairly simple proposition. The most primitive and easiest way to make cheese is simply to milk a goat or cow, then let the lactic acid bacteria that are naturally present in the milk take over. They will eventually produce enough acid to exclude many harmful organisms and to thicken the milk into a simple cultured milk product or a cheese. This process was clearly illustrated to me when a student of mine gave me a jar of fresh, unpasteurized goat's milk. At the time, I had no idea of what to do with it and carelessly let it sit at room temperature for a few days. Much to my surprise, when I opened the jar to take a look at its contents, it had turned to a thick, cream-cheese-like texture with a wonderful acidic "bite."

Now you may think that was a foolish or dangerous thing to do. I was eating spoiled milk, after all. But you should understand that many types of bacteria are found in fresh, clean milk, and those that produce lactic acid as a by-product of their metabolism (and that can survive and thrive in an acid medium) will quickly take over. The more acid they produce, the less likely "putrefactive" bacteria, which don't do well in an acid environment, are to survive and proliferate. In addition, the more acidic the milk becomes, the more the proteins in it tend to curdle. This is the simple process through which we get cream cheese, sour cream, buttermilk, crème fraîche, yogurt, and so on, depending upon which kind of acid-producing bacteria are present in the milk and how the milk is handled.

The second way to produce simple cheeses is to add some kind of acid to them. Instead of waiting for the bacteria to take over slowly, we hurry things up by adding a substantial quantity of acid all at one time. Lemon juice, vinegar, and even buttermilk (with its high acid content) have been used to coagulate or thicken milk. The ricotta cheese recipe in this chapter is designed to illustrate just such a principle.

Now let's suppose that you don't have quick and easy access to a cow or goat. Let's suppose that you need to rely upon a farmer who may live 50 miles from your home, and that it takes him two days to get the fresh milk to you. Under less than sanitary or optimum conditions of storage and transport, decay-causing bacteria may get a hold in the milk and proliferate, and you, upon drinking it, could get sick. With the advent of big cities, this became a problem for the people living in them. Milk was essentially an unsafe product to drink. (There is a vivid opening scene in *A Tale of Two Cities* where a nobleman's carriage carrying wine barrels overturns on a Paris street. The barrels are broken and their contents spill out into the street. The poor of the area scramble with whatever containers they can find to salvage some of the precious wine. A mother dips the hem of her skirt in the wine to absorb as much as possible and then squeezes the contents of the skirt into the mouth of her hungry infant. We might feel that wine is wholly unsuitable for an infant to consume and that he ought to be drinking milk, but wine was a safe product in those days, incapable of poisoning anyone because of its high alcohol content, and milk was not!)

What's the solution? How do you make milk safe for the consumer who may live far from the farm? A large part of the question was answered by Louis Pasteur, who discovered that heating the milk to a certain temperature for a certain length of time would kill all bacteria, both useful and harmful, and that the milk would be free of bacteria and decay for a period of time. Today most of the milk available is pasteurized. If we wish to make a cultured milk product from pasteurized milk, we must add our own bacterial culture.

A third and slightly more complicated type of fresh cheese involves introducing a bacterial culture to acidify the milk, then adding a nip of rennet to coagulate it more solidly. The curds or protein parts of the milk will solidify, and the whey or liquid portions will separate from them. We then drain the whey from the curds and are left with a nice little cheese. The recipes for chèvre and fromage blanc in this chapter, which use the New England Cheesemaking Supply Company's simple bacteria-and-rennet cultures, are designed to illustrate this type of cheese.

PREPARING TO MAKE CHEESE

Absolute cleanliness at each step along the way is imperative. All aspects of handling milk must be absolutely sanitary: the dairy and milking stands, the dairy person, the equipment of both the cheesemaker and the dairy, you, the kitchen, and all the equipment. If everything involved in the process is not absolutely clean, you run the risk of contaminating your cheese with bacteria that may either cause the cheese to spoil or be harmful to you. So your first step in making cheese should be to sanitize your work area and equipment. (My neighbor, Ernest, a pathologist, once re-marked how clean my kitchen sink was, and understood immedi-ately when I quipped "This is my lab, Ernest!") I sanitize my sink and counters by using a solution of water and chlorine bleach. I then sterilize all equipment I intend to use (thermometer, small wire whisk, spoons, sponges, and hands) by giving them a soak in the "soup"—a solution of 2 tablespoons liquid household bleach in about a sinkful of water. After removing them, I rinse them thor-oughly (any remaining bleach could kill your cheese culture) and set them on a very clean towel.

The next step is to decide whether or not you intend to pas-teurize your milk. Officially, you should pasteurize all milk before making cheese. So officially, that's what I'm recommending. By pasteurizing your milk, you kill most bacteria present, both harm-ful and beneficial, and you can then introduce the bacteria of your choosing where it will be able to grow unmolested. I'd like to mention, however, that in France, goat and sheep's milk cheese are never pasteurized, owing to their naturally low bacterial count. Noted French cheese expert Pierre Androuet states his be-lief that farmhouse cheeses made from raw milk "*sont la verité du terroir*" (are the very heart of the land). While Mexican cooking aficionada Diana Kennedy says that she thinks the Mexican style cheeses made in the United States taste "insipid . . . owing no doubt to the pasteurized milk." I have made cheeses both ways and have found the differences to be more textural than in taste. If you choose to pasteurize your milk, you may do so easily by using what the California State Department of Health refers to as the "high temperature/short time" method of pasteurization. Bring the milk to 161°F for 15 seconds, then cool very quickly. If you choose to leave it unpasteurized, remember to make sure the milk comes from goats that are checked regularly for disease, that the dairy is impec-cably clean, and that you and your kitchen are as well. I usually use "certified" raw goat's milk available at my local health food store.

Probably the other most important factor to consider before

making your cheese is the quality of the milk itself. Just as you can't make good wine from lousy grapes, so you can't make a good cheese from milk of inferior quality. You may have little control over the quality of milk you can find unless you raise your own goats, but at least you should know a bit about the factors affecting flavor. The time of year, the quality and nature of the feed, the physical and emotional state of the goat (remember the old Carnation motto "milk from contented cows"?), the breed of the goat . . . all affect the quality of the milk.

Madeleine Kamman, in her book on the regional cooking of Savoie, underscores the importance of feed in producing good milk when she says the "*maître berger* (master or head shepherd) was responsible for alternating the grazing of the animals, one day in a patch of grassy plants, the next in a patch of leguminous plants." She further tells us that "the thickness and richness of the milk depended entirely on his knowledge of the terrain and the plants growing in the meadows." The French statesman Talleyrand proclaimed his belief that nothing could compare to "*le brie au regain*" or Brie from a cow pastured on second-growth grasses. And the well-known French purveyor of quality cheese, Pierre Androuet, says he considers the flowering of the fields the supreme moment of pasturage. My friend Carole Saville, who once owned a herd of Nubian goats, says she always intended to plant a field of thyme and lavender for them to graze on in order to improve the flavor of her already good cheeses.

Making Yogurt

In Greece, as in many countries where it is popular, yogurt is often made from goat's milk. A goat's milk yogurt is often thicker and richer than that made from cow's milk, and sometimes a bit more piquant. Here is the simple, old-fashioned way to make yogurt. Heat a gallon of the milk to the boiling point. Allow it to cool to about 120°F. (I use either a dairy thermometer or an instant-read thermometer, available at most cookware shops, to measure temperature for making yogurt and cheese.) Then add a few tablespoons of store-bought plain yogurt and stir it in. Make sure to purchase plain yogurt from a store with a rapid turnover. Pour the milk and yogurt into a bowl, cover with a plate, and allow the mixture to stand in a warm place for several hours. A temperature of 110°F is optimum for incubation of your yogurt, so try to ensure that the yogurt is kept as close as possible to this temperature for several hours. Here are several ways to do it:

- Set it in the sun on a warm day (the obvious, very old-fashioned way).

- Leave it in the oven with a pilot light on (or if you don't have a pilot light, rig up a light bulb for warmth).

- Wrap it in your down jacket.

- Wrap it in a towel and put it on a heating pad on the low setting.

- Incubate it in a wide-mouthed thermos.

- Buy a yogurt maker.

When your yogurt appears to have turned from milk into yogurt (usually 4 to 6 hours) put it in the refrigerator. The longer it incubates, the more tart it becomes. The beauty of homemade yogurt to me is that it is often more delicate and mild than the store-bought variety. For added calcium and body, you can add ½ cup of noninstant powdered milk to your milk before incubating it.

Two Cheese Recipes

The only special equipment you need to make these simple cheeses is a dairy or instant-read thermometer, which can be purchased at most gourmet cookware shops, and some cheesecloth. The ricotta cheese recipe uses buttermilk to acidify the milk, the fromage blanc or chèvre requires the use of a culture.

Goat's Milk Ricotta Cheese

The ricotta cheese you can make at home is far more delicate in flavor than what you buy at the grocery store, and its texture is delightful. Making ricotta cheese is very simple; it's an excellent cheese for a beginner because it's almost impossible to mess up if you follow a few simple instructions.

> 1 gallon whole or   1 quart cultured buttermilk
>   low fat goat's milk

1. In a large pot, heat the milk to about 180°F.
2. When the milk reaches 180°F, add the buttermilk. Turn off heat. Stir gently a few times and watch the curd begin to form.
3. When the curds (the solid portion) and the whey (the liquid) have separated and the whey is almost clear (about 10 minutes), pour them into a strainer lined with cheesecloth and allow the cheese to drain for about an hour.
4. Place the cheese in a bowl and refrigerate for a couple of hours before using.
5. Use in any recipe that calls for ricotta cheese. A delicate fresh cheese such as this should be used within a day or two.

Makes about 4 cups.

Fromage Blanc or Chèvre

Fromage blanc and chèvre are simple fresh cheeses, somewhat similar in texture to cream cheese, which can be used by themselves or as a base for the flavored spreads at the end of the chapter. If you are watching your fat intake, you can make these cheeses with low-fat milk with equally good results. You will need what is called a direct set culture, a simple invention of the New England Cheesemaking Supply Company that includes a bacterial culture and a bit of rennet in one packet. (The "Sources" list at the end of this book gives their address.) Each packet comes with the instructions printed on it, but they run pretty much like this:

1 gallon fresh goat's milk	1 packet Chèvre or Fromage Blanc Direct Set Culture

If you are using pasteurized milk (or wish to pasteurize your raw milk), heat it to about 180°F, then quickly cool it to the appropriate temperature. (The appropriate temperature is different for each of the cultures. See the packets for details.) To cool the milk quickly, pour it into a bowl and place the bowl in a sinkful of ice. When the milk reaches the right temperature, add the starter culture, cover the bowl with plastic wrap, and allow it to incubate at room temperature until the curds and whey separate. Then pour the curds into a strainer lined with cheesecloth or into small plastic cheese molds (available from the New England Cheesemaking Supply Company) and allow it to drain overnight. Unmold your cheeses and roll them in fresh chopped chives, salt and pepper, or mix your cheese with the flavorings suggested in the recipes that follow and use them as spreads.

Use your fresh cheese within a week, or freeze it for later use. It will keep in the freezer for up to a month.

Makes about 4 cups.

Cheese Spreads

Your fromage blanc or chèvre can serve as the basis for a number of delicious spreads. Here are a few of my favorites.

Olive–Goat Cheese Spread

Fresh goat cheese is best appreciated as is, but I find this particular recipe irresistible. I love it for an afternoon snack or an appetizer on crackers with a glass of champagne!

16 ounces freshly made goat cheese
Garlic to taste
⅔ cup grated sharp white Cheddar

Some fresh thyme, chopped parsley, or basil
¼ to ½ cup chopped pitted home-cured olives (see Chapter 1)

1. Using a food processor, thoroughly mix the goat cheese, garlic, Cheddar, and herbs.
2. Toss in the chopped olives and pulse just until they are mixed in with the other ingredients. (If you let the machine run any longer, you will have a purple cheese, which isn't so bad. I just happen to prefer fairly large chunks of olive in my cheese.)
3. Refrigerate overnight and serve at room temperature.

Makes 3 cups.

Mock Boursin

Boursin is a fresh French cream cheese. It is usually flavored with garlic and fresh herbs and can often be purchased at specialty cheese shops. You can make it yourself using either cow or goat cheese. Boursin is best when made with fresh herbs, never dried!

2 cloves fresh garlic
16 ounces freshly
   made cream cheese
   or goat cheese
½ cup finely chopped
   fresh chives

½ cup chopped parsley
Any of fresh herbs you
   wish in any amounts
   you wish (such as
   fresh thyme, basil,
   oregano, etc.)

1. Press the garlic with a garlic press and add to the cheese. Whirl the mixture in the food processor until thoroughly blended.

2. Add chives, parsley, and any other herbs. Blend until the herbs and cheese are a consistency that suits you.

3. Pack the cheese into a crock or container and refrigerate for several hours until the flavors blend. Can be stored for up to 1 week in the refrigerator.

Makes about 2 cups.

Fiesta Spread

This delightful cheese spread is a bit too runny to be easily formed into a cheese ball, so I generally serve it in a crock. Using goat cheese gives it a more interesting flavor than store-bought cream cheese.

1 small container of
   fresh "mild" salsa,
   very well drained
12 ounces freshly made
   goat cheese or
   cream cheese

1 cup grated very
   sharp Cheddar
Several sprigs fresh
   cilantro

1. Drain the small container of salsa thoroughly in a strainer. Be sure to press out as much juice as possible.

2. Blend the cheese and Cheddar in the workbowl of a food processor until thoroughly mixed.

3. Add the well-drained salsa and the fresh cilantro sprigs and blend just until mixed thoroughly. Do not make a paste of this stuff; leave some texture.

4. Refrigerate for a few hours to allow the flavors to blend, then serve at room temperature with crackers.

Makes about 2 cups.

Blue Cheese–Garlic Herb Spread

This spread seems to suit nearly everyone well—blue cheese lovers, garlic lovers, and herb cheese lovers! It is a very strongly flavored blend, so watch out . . . and feel free to vary the quantities to suit your personal taste.

2 to 3 cloves garlic	4 ounces blue cheese
16 ounces freshly made	(more or less to taste)
goat cheese or	Any chopped fresh herbs
cream cheese	that suit you (rosemary,
	thyme, lemon thyme,
	chives, sage, etc.)

1. Using a garlic press, press the fresh garlic, add to the cream cheese, and blend thoroughly in the workbowl of the food processor.

2. Add the blue cheese, broken into chunks, and the herbs. Blend only until the blue cheese is well broken up and the herbs are mixed in.

3. Pack cheese into a crock or container and refrigerate for several hours until the flavors blend. (This cheese is a bit runny for forming into a ball, but it can be done.)

Makes about 2½ cups.

A Goat Cheese Menu

Assorted Flavored Goat Cheese Spreads and Crackers

🌿

Salade Mesclun with Fresh Goat Cheese Rounds,
Hazelnut Oil, and Raspberry Vinegar

🌿

Grilled Leg of Lamb in Provençal Marinade

🌿

Garlic, Herb, and Chèvre Mashed Potatoes

🌿

Green Beans Drizzled with Basil Oil, Sun-Dried
Tomatoes, Crumbled Chèvre, and Toasted Pine Nuts

🌿

Lemon Yogurt Cake with Whipped Yogurt
Topping and Fresh Berries

🌿

Suggested Wines:
Sancerre or fumé blanc (with appetizers or salad)

Cabernet sauvignon or Bordeaux with the main entrée

California late-harvest sauvignon blanc
or a good Sauterne (with dessert)

I can never get enough goat cheese. This simple menu reflects my
love of it, and as soon as I figure out how to make *crottin* (a hard,
dry French goat cheese), it, too, will be added to my repertoire.
Laura Chenel, California goat cheese goddess, has written a
book chock-full of recipes using all kinds of chèvre entitled simply *Chèvre! The Goat Cheese Cookbook.* I highly recommend it.

Salade Mesclun with Fresh Goat Cheese Rounds, Hazelnut Oil, and Raspberry Vinegar

This salad is delicious. During the holiday season, you might consider making a cranberry vinegar to use in place of the raspberry vinegar suggested here. And if you are watching calories, leave out the hazelnut oil. You'll find the raspberry vinegar has so much flavor all by itself that the oil won't be missed.

4 cups mesclun or
    mixed greens
8 rounds of goat cheese
½ cup Raspberry
    Vinegar (see Chapter 4)

¼ cup Hazelnut
    Oil (see Chapter 7)
¼ cup chopped
    hazelnuts, lightly toasted

1. Divide the greens among 4 plates.
2. Place 2 slices of goat cheese on each plate.
3. Drizzle 2 tablespoons of raspberry vinegar and 1 tablespoon of hazelnut oil over each salad. Sprinkle one tablespoon of chopped hazelnuts over each salad. Keep them separate to get the full color and flavor impact; do not mix them together as you might an ordinary oil and vinegar.

Makes 4 servings.

Grilled Leg of Lamb in Provençal Marinade

Get a butterflied leg of lamb from a first-rate butcher, then marinate it for at least 24 hours in this hearty marinade made of homemade red wine vinegar and fresh herbes de Provence.

½ cup Basic Country-
Style Mustard (see
Chapter 3), or
Dijon-style mustard
¼ cup homemade red
wine vinegar (see
Chapter 4)

¼ cup fresh lemon juice
6 cloves fresh garlic
½ cup olive oil
¼ cup fresh herbes de
Provence (see Chapter 2)

1. Combine all ingredients except herbes de Provence in a blender and whirl until smooth.

2. Add the herbs to the blender and mix in.

3. Marinate lamb overnight and grill over medium-hot coals for about 20 minutes on each side (or until done the way you like it).

Makes 4 servings.

Garlic, Herb, and Chèvre
Mashed Potatoes

If I am a bit vague or loose about the amounts in this recipe, it is simply because I always wing this one, adding whatever happens to appeal to me on any given day. They are inevitably delicious, but then potatoes are my favorite food anyway. Here is a rough approximation of what I like in them best. You can make these up a day ahead of time for a party and just heat them before serving.

3 large potatoes
4 ounces very sharp
Cheddar, grated
1 cup homemade chèvre
or fromage blanc
1 cup sour cream
1 tablespoon Society
Garlic Blend
(see Chapter 7)

3 cloves fresh garlic,
pressed through
a garlic press
A few tablespoons of milk
Salt and pepper to taste

1. Preheat oven to 350°F. Boil potatoes until tender, then mash the remaining ingredients with them.

2. Place mashed potatoes in the oven until heated through (20 to 30 minutes).

Makes 4 servings.

Green Beans Drizzled with Basil Oil, Sun-Dried Tomatoes, Chèvre, and Toasted Pine Nuts

If you have never had just-picked Blue Lake beans (the most flavorful, in my opinion), you haven't lived! Each year, it is a race with my bunny to see which of us can get to the green beans first. Cooking them by the simple French method retains color and flavor best of all. Simply bring a large pot of water to a boil, then drop your beans into it whole. Allow them to cook for 3 to 5 minutes (until tender), then drain them and pour icy water over them to stop the cooking action quickly. Place them on a platter and serve at room temperature, drizzled with Basil Oil (see Chapter 7), and sprinkled with thinly sliced sun-dried tomatoes, crumbled chèvre, freshly toasted pine nuts, and chopped scallions.

Lemon Yogurt Cake with Whipped Yogurt Topping and Fresh Berries

Yogurt cake is a popular Greek dessert with the flavor and texture of a rich pound cake. This one is topped with a sweetened, whipped homemade yogurt topping (which is amazingly delicious, even when made with nonfat yogurt) and berries or other fresh fruit.

1¾ cups yogurt	3 cups flour
¾ cup (1½ sticks) butter	Pinch salt
1½ cups sugar	2 teaspoons baking powder
2 tablespoons grated	¾ teaspoon baking soda
lemon zest	Whipped Yogurt Topping
3 eggs	Fresh berries

1. Preheat oven to 350°F. Grease a couple of "Texas size" muffin tins or a 9-by-13-inch baking pan. Hang the yogurt in some cheesecloth or place in a yogurt strainer and allow to drain for about 20 minutes.

2. In the workbowl of a food processor or mixer, cream butter, sugar, and lemon zest. Drop eggs through the feed tube, one at a time, and mix until thoroughly incorporated.

3. Mix flour, salt, baking powder, and baking soda together. Remove the lid from the food processor and dump the flour mixture in. Process just until mixed in thoroughly.

4. Add lightly drained yogurt and pulse just until blended.

5. Pour the cake batter into prepared muffin tins or baking pan and bake for about an hour or until a toothpick comes out clean.

6. Slice a muffin or piece of cake in half and top each half with some of the Whipped Yogurt Topping and some fresh raspberries, blackberries, or other fruit in season.

FOR WHIPPED YOGURT TOPPING:

Drain 2 cups cold goat yogurt lightly in a piece of cheesecloth or a yogurt strainer for about 20 minutes. Whip the lightly drained yogurt and a tablespoon or two of sugar with a hand-held electric mixer or a whisk until its volume is increased a bit and its texture is similar to that of lightly whipped cream. Spoon a dollop on each slice of cake.

Makes about 12 servings.

CHAPTER 6

Just Plain Bread

 EACH YEAR, the San Diego Museum of Man hosts a Native American festival where Native American artisans and craftsmen from throughout the Southwest come to sell their wares and show their crafts. I went to it a few years ago, with the idea of buying some of the simple yet elegant silverwork for which the Native Americans of the southwestern United States are so famous. I found my silver, but I also found something else. Tucked away in a corner of the museum courtyard was an old Hopi woman making piki bread. Piki bread is simply a watery, thin mixture of blue cornmeal and water, spread across a flat baking stone over a fire and cooked until dry. The very thin sheet is then removed from the stone, rolled up, as if it were a scroll, and sold to the highest bidder. "This is for me," I thought, as I sank down on my haunches and settled in for a lengthy squat. I must have sat silently watching for 20 or 30 minutes. Tourists came and tourists went, many taking with them piki bread to try. Finally, after perhaps a half an hour had passed, without any introduction, she began to speak to me. She didn't look at me. She didn't introduce herself. She simply began to speak as if she had finally decided that any Anglo who

was willing to sit quietly and watch for that long without asking annoying questions, deserved some kind of a "bone." She described how they initiated young girls into her tribe, a sort of coming of age ceremony. Each young girl, she explained, when she comes of age, spends four days in complete ceremonial dark, grinding corn—no speaking, no light, just the girl and the corn. As I listened I realized I was standing in the face of an awesome and almost worldwide reverence for the connection between the fertile forces of nature (specifically bread) and woman.

Wherever you look, whether in the Mediterranean or the Americas, you will find someone celebrating this intimate connection in one way or another. To the Egyptians, it was Isis who taught men to cultivate grain. To the Greeks, it was Demeter. To the ancient Sumerians, holy Ninlil was the goddess who gave the gift of grain and was keeper of the divine grain chamber of the heavens. To the Romans, it was Ceres. The Romans even had a goddess of the oven, Fornax, with her own annual feast, the Fornacalia, celebrated each year on June 9. True, the professional bakers of the world have generally been men, but the givers of agriculture and the domestic bakers of bread, the practitioners of the "lost art" of baking in the home, are women.

Choosing Grains for Bread

The major pockets of civilization in the Western world originally grew up where there were supplies of wild grasses and grains. People ate them and then just moved on to greener pastures. Then one day, someone got the bright idea to plant seeds and stick around to eat the results, and thus began agriculture, which eventually formed the basis of what we call Western civilization. As more and more sophisticated techniques of cultivating and utilizing grain developed, populations grew and "civilization" developed as humans freed themselves from the constant need of foraging to survive.

As a home baker, perhaps the most dedicated thing you can do is grow your own grain. What a great idea! A regional magazine did a feature not long ago on how you can grow your own wheat at home, thresh it with a simple procedure called the "tennis shoe stomp" (a term and technique developed by Rosalind Creasy), then grind it and bake it into the finest loaf of whole wheat "home grown" you've ever sunk your teeth into. But few of us are willing to go that far, at least on a regular basis. So the next best thing, in my estimation, is to buy whole grains, grind them fresh yourself in a home mill, freeze what you don't use in reclosable freezer bags, and then bake at your leisure.

If you want to bake wheat bread, it's hard winter or hard spring wheat you want. The "hard" simply denotes grain with a high gluten content, which is desirable in bread flour, since carbon dioxide bubbles trapped in between the fibers of gluten are what gives bread its rise. You can purchase hard red wheat berries or hard white wheat berries (with slight variations in color) at many health food stores or by mail order (see "Sources" at the end of the book).

If you want whole wheat pastry flour, purchase soft spring wheat; the "soft" lets you know that the grain contains less gluten, making it more suitable for cookies, quick breads, biscuits, muffins, and so on. If you want cornbread, buy organically grown corn and grind your own. (Never use feed corn or seed corn, which may have been treated with god-knows-what and will most assuredly be inferior in flavor and texture to organic corn grown for human consumption.) I nearly always add some organically grown unbleached white bread flour to my whole-grain breads to "lighten" the texture of the finished product.

Wheat has always been the number one choice of bakers throughout the ages for leavened bread because of its significant gluten content, but rye (originally a weed in the wheat fields) has also been valued. It, too, contains some gluten. Oats, millet, and barley have all been used to sustain life in the Old World, but because they contain little or no gluten, they are not of much value in baking leavened breads, except as interesting textural and nutritional additives. They have often been made into porridge or gruel for those who couldn't afford or didn't possess the technology to bake leavened breads. One of my favorite quotes comes from Sir Alfred Zimmern, who characterized the typical Attican evening meal during ancient times as being "of two courses: the first a kind of porridge, and the second, a kind of porridge."

WHERE TO BUY GRAINS

You can often buy small quantities of whole grains at your local health food store (mine stocks all kinds in bulk bins), or you can order them by mail from one of the sources listed at the end of the book. Shipping costs for larger quantities, however, are often fairly high. To circumvent the problem, let your local health food store place the order for you. They will get the grain from a distributor who makes weekly deliveries, saving you the shipping costs.

Milling Grains at Home

Consider what our ancestors had to go through to mill their grains in even the crudest of senses. A mythical he or she might have said, "This stuff sure fills the old bread hole, but chewing it's a real annoyance! Cracks your teeth. Gets stuck in 'em. Takes so dang long. Wonder if I squashed it up first," and he or she promptly found a couple of solid rocks to squash a few grains between, and then found out if you soak them in addition to squashing them, you really had something! Here was bread at its beginnings. Mush. And that tends to be what primitive peoples ate: mush. The Roman armies marched on mush. The legendary Spartan warriors ate mush. The Greek man-on-the-street ate mush. And, unbeknownst to the European populace, what do you suppose the inhabitants of the New World were eating for breakfast, lunch, and dinner? That's right: *cornmeal* mush.

Next step? Heat it up a bit, then let it sit around for a while, or better yet, cook it on a flat stone, like my Native American friend with her piki bread. Then you've got something even better than mush. You've got flatbread, vestiges of which are alive and well and popping up in cuisines all over the world today: the corn tortilla and Hopi piki bread, for instance, in the Americas; the pita breads of Mediterranean cuisine; the chapati and parathas of the Indian subcontinent; the Chinese pancake, to name a few.

Rotary hand mills were eventually developed, and then, a large-scale mill that could be powered either by slaves or by some poor hapless animal doomed to spend its life walking in circles, dragging a millstone. The advantages were that fairly large quantities of grain could be ground in fairly short periods of time. The disadvantages were that you sometimes got sand in your flour, the miller could easily cheat you out of some of your grain (millers were notoriously unpopular in the Middle Ages for this reason), and at any moment, the mill might inexplicably explode, leaving the surrounding inhabitants with the distinct impression that the devil was at work in the mill. (The modern miller is aware that as soon as more than 20 grams of flour dust are distributed in each square yard of air, there is danger of explosion set off by the frictional heat of grinding.) Mills were later powered by water (freeing the poor animals to work elsewhere) and by wind!

But none of this helps us grind our flour at home, does it? What to do? Well, there are any number of mills on the market today designed specifically for use in the home. Some of them are stone mills, while some contain steel parts. Some of them can be powered by hand, some are electric. Some are slow, and some are fast. But the best and most efficient available is made by the Magic Mill/Nutriplex Corporation of Salt Lake City, Utah. It isn't cheap (retails for about $300). But it is probably the quickest and most efficient mill on the market and will last a lifetime. (My only complaint is that it sounds a lot like an airplane at takeoff. I just wear earplugs when using it.) And if you have never smelled the wonderful, sweet, nutty aroma of freshly ground wheat berries, you just haven't lived! A few minutes each month wearing earplugs and I have enough fragrant, freshly ground wheat and corn to freeze and last for a month or two. (Even when frozen, my freshly ground flour outdistances by far anything you can buy in a market or health food store in terms of flavor, texture, and aroma.) Occasionally I grind oats and rye, just to have a bit of both kinds of flour on hand for special needs.

Leavening

Think for a moment about what people did before the advent of commercial yeast. In most cases, they just mixed flour of some kind with water and waited around for any wild yeasts lurking in the air to take up residence in the flour and make it rise magically. When they got lucky and the dough rose, they would save a small piece of it and use it to inoculate the next day's bread with the appropriate organisms. This is spontaneously leavened bread, or *pain au levain,* as the French call it. You can use the same technique today if you have the patience and time. You can mix water with flour and wait around for wild yeasts and local bacteria to populate your blend. They will eventually proliferate and produce a "mother" or "starter" which you can then use to leaven and flavor bread. It is not always as reliable and successful as making bread using commercial yeast, but it is worth the effort if you are really interested in bread and its beginnings. I have included instructions for making *pain au levain* if you would like to try experimenting along those lines.

The commercial yeasts which we use today are simply modern man's way of speeding up the process. They consist of some highly reliable strains of yeast in a concentrated source that will quickly produce the rise we need in our dough.

When choosing a commercial yeast for your bread, I suggest you avoid the so-called "rapid-rise" types of yeast. Rapid-rise-type yeasts tend to turn a molehill into a mountain in a matter of minutes. Big, gaping bubbles appear, and the whole process is just a little too close to the "microwave dinner" mentality for my taste. Really good bread takes time. Any of the non-rapid-rise types of yeast from either a grocery or health food store should do a better job. Check the expiration date on the package to be sure you are not using yeast that has lost its potency. We "proof" yeast (mix it in warm water) before adding it to the bread dough partly to check that it is still active. The appearance of bubbles on the surface of the water within 10 to 15 minutes after you have stirred it in tells you that your yeast is alive and well. Williams-Sonoma stocks a particularly active brand of French baker's yeast (saf-instant brand) which I prefer to use. It can even be mixed directly into the dough without proofing or dissolving in water if you so desire. It gives excellent loft without all those air bubbles and will lift even the heaviest of whole-grain breads.

Mixing Your Dough

One Sunday morning, I arrived at 5 A.M. to spend my day with the baker at a well-known Italian bakery. The baker was Mexican with a smattering of English at his command. He had been trained by the founding corps of Italian bakers, who then moved on to corporate headquarters, leaving Jose to mind the store. Jose was more than gracious and delighted to have someone take such an interest in his métier. And between my very rudimentary Spanish and his far better command of English, and both of our enthusiastic spirits, we managed to have a fine morning of baking and learning. One thing I remember him stressing at the time came back to haunt me later. He said the secret was in the mixing of the dough.

And at the time, I thought, "Yeah, yeah," and let it go at that.

In retrospect, it was then that I began to realize that the way in which you mix your dough may indeed make a distinct difference in the end product. Nearly all professional bakers use some kind of machine to mix their doughs, even if they finish them by hand, so it seems to me that the extra power offered by a really good mechanical mixer might give a more interesting texture to the finished product. (I often made my doughs in a professional-sized Cuisinart food processor, and the thing I hated most was the incredible mess it made and the heck of a time I had cleaning dough out of all those nooks and crannies. Then there was the fact that sometimes the motor would overheat fairly quickly and shut off.) I was particularly impressed with a demonstration I saw of a Bosch mixer. It was being used to mix a whole-grain dough, and it just kept on working and working and working until that dough was the smoothest, most elastic piece of dough I had ever seen! In addition, the finished loaf, which was made entirely of whole grains, was about the lightest loaf I could have imagined.

Once again, the Magic Mill/Nutriplex Corporation came to the rescue with a Swedish-made machine, similar to the Bosch, which they had only recently begun to carry, called the Magic Mill DLX 9000 Kitchen Machine. It was designed in Sweden after a machine professional bakers use and seems to develop gluten in a way that nothing else can. It has a powerful motor that just never stops working, is very easy to clean, and can easily process up to 15 pounds of dough (25 cups of flour) at one time. The machine does its kneading with a roller rather than a dough hook (which sometimes tears the dough) and was designed to simulate the action of human knuckles on the dough. It may sound a bit goofy, but it works beautifully. You can easily dump additional ingredients like nuts, fruits, flour, or whatever into the dough while the machine is running. I have really enjoyed using it and would recommend that anyone thinking of purchasing a useful mixing and kneading machine for bread baking consider looking into this one. Like anything of quality, the machine is not cheap (it retails for close to $475) but it is virtually indestructible, highly useful, and should last a lifetime.

Bread on the Rise

The period of time when the bread is rising is a crucial one. This is the time when the bread develops all its interesting nuances of flavor (provided you have used good grain in the first place). It is also the period of time when the bread develops its characteristic loft.

Kneading the bread develops long, elastic strands of a protein present in flour called gluten. The rise comes from a simple reaction. As the yeast eats the complex carbohydrates in the bread, it gives off carbon dioxide gas. The carbon dioxide given off by the yeast is then trapped between the strands of gluten, causing the bread to rise or, in a sense, to inflate.

The process of flavor developing in bread can be likened in many ways to what happens in a batch of wine as it is fermenting and aging. New chemicals bond with one another, old bonds break, and new and interesting flavors develop as a result. Remember the primary rule: a long, slow rise develops a more interesting flavor than a "quickie" does. Leave nature to its own devices, give chemical reactions time to occur, and you will get a superior flavor.

Cookbooks have a tendency to specify the precise amount of time your bread should take to rise. This is not always practical or helpful. You, for instance, might wish to mix a dough tonight but bake it tomorrow morning for breakfast. What happens when your recipe specifies that the first rise should take place within an hour or an hour and a half? Will you have to get up at 3:00 A.M. in order to mix your dough and give it its requisite hour-and-a-half rise? Most assuredly not. You can mix it the night before and consign it to the refrigerator until a more reasonable hour of the morning. The cold of the refrigerator will not only have slowed down the action of the yeast, but it will also have afforded the bread time to develop complexities of flavor which it might not otherwise possess. (Optimum temperature for yeast development is 80°F.)

The dough is forgiving. Use the times suggested in your recipes as guides as you are learning to bake bread. Then, as you begin to develop a feel for the dough, adapt and vary your recipes to suit your needs, learn to tell when the dough has risen suffi- ciently by the way it looks and feels rather than by the times sug- gested in the book. (On a warm day, your dough will rise more rapidly; on a cold day, more slowly.) There are two methods used by experienced bakers to tell whether a dough has risen suffi- ciently. One method is to wait for the dough to double in volume. However, since you may not always be able to tell when the dough has doubled in volume, an even better method is to stick your fin- ger into it. If the indentation made by your finger stays and the dough feels light and airy, it is probably ready to be shaped into a loaf. The amount of time your dough takes to get to that stage will vary according to the temperature of the room and of your ingre- dients, the strength of your yeast and the quality of the flour used. It cannot always be measured in precise segments of time.

Shaping the Dough

When I was growing up, a loaf of bread was precisely that—a loaf, shaped like a rectangular loaf pan. It never occurred to me that a loaf of bread might come in any other form. Even bread that my mother bought weekly from a nearby Danish bakery was al- ways a rectangular loaf. And once again, the first time it occurred to me that bread might take a different form was in good old Berkeley. The Cheese Board began to carry unusual (to me) shapes of bread to go with its vast selection of cheeses. And a shop out on Solano Avenue was baking round loaves filled with herbs and cheeses! This was a big revelation to me. Today, I very rarely bake bread in a loaf pan. I prefer to shape it by hand because I like the feel of the dough and I enjoy the very rustic-looking finish I get with a freestanding loaf of bread.

I generally bake round or oblong-shaped loaves these days, and I vary the design by varying the slash-mark patterns on their tops or dusting them with flour. Here are my favorite shapes and slash mark patterns:

Describing how to shape a loaf of bread to someone who has never done it before is a little like trying to teach someone how to ski by telling them about it! It's much easier to show them. It's much easier to work with them, side by side, step by step, and show how its done. However, I am convinced that anyone who every played with clay as a child (and who didn't?) can use those remembered experiences to shape bread. Remember when you rolled clay snakes? Well, making a baguette is a lot like rolling a snake. And didn't you ever just roll a nice piece of clay into a smooth ball? Well shaping a round loaf of bread is a lot like making a clay ball. Your first efforts may be a bit embarrassing, but if you stick to it, you will eventually produce something of which you can be proud.

You need to pay attention to what you are doing and have fun with it. To shape a loaf, gently press all the air out of the risen dough. If you want a round loaf of bread, fold the edges underneath the loaf and gently roll it until it is smooth on top. All loaves of bread shaped in this way will have a top side that is fairly smooth and an underside with wrinkles on it! If you want a baguette, roll out a rectangular piece of dough with a rolling pin, then roll it up by hand into a "snake" (like you would a jelly roll). If you want an oblong loaf of greater width than the traditional baguette, fold under two sides of a circular disk of dough and then gently shape it as you wish. When you have finally achieved the shape you desire, place it on your baker's peel dusted with cornmeal, cover it with plastic wrap or a damp tea towel, and allow it to rise until it is light, doubled in bulk, and ready to bake.

SLASHING THE LOAF

Just before you put the bread in the oven, you will need to slash it in several places across the top to enhance its appearance, and to ensure that the gases that escape during the baking process will do so in a predictable manner rather than by tearing your loaf in a random pattern. Some books suggest you do your slashing with a razor blade, but I find a sharp, serrated knife easier to handle. Slash fairly deeply so that the grooves remain intact during the baking process.

Baking Your Bread

I'm a big oven fan. And, probably like most people who decide to take bread seriously, I have a fantasy of building a wonderful wood-burning, rustic brick oven down on the "back forty" (that is, of course, as soon as I get a back forty!). I can hear the crackling of crusts and smell the hickory or cedar smoke, and I can taste the fully developed flavors of the pizzas and breads I will bake in my oven. For the time being, I content myself with looking at pictures of ovens in all sorts of books and reading about them.

What an ingenious invention the oven is! They say that the Egyptians were the first ones to really get onto the idea and do something with it. They also say that the Egyptians built conical ovens with two chambers, a lower one for the fire and an upper chamber for the breads, which of necessity had to be small because the ovens never seemed to accumulate enough heat to cook large wads of dough thoroughly. (I suspect the beehive oven of today found in some of the more rural areas of the world is a vestige of such an oven. Some visiting Soviet Georgian chefs once described to me the way rustic breads are baked in their country. The oven has its heat source and baking area all in one chamber, and the raw dough is simply slapped onto the wall of the oven until it cooks and is about ready to fall off.)

The Greeks further developed the oven, then brought it to Rome with them, where the Romans made a religion and an art of it. The amazing thing is that no one seemed to think of venting an oven until nearly the 18th century! While looking at a photo recently of an Indian *horno* or earthen oven on a Taos Pueblo reservation, I began to wonder how the oven developed in the Americas and realized that it didn't really, at least not in the southwestern United States, until the Spanish conquerors introduced it to the native inhabitants, who then gave it their own twist.

Perhaps one of the most ingenious "ovens" I've discovered to date was described to me by a young Taiwanese student of mine. "Jimmy's" dad taught him how to build a very primitive type of oven for use on family jaunts to the cemetery. (Many traditional Chinese follow the ancient custom of bringing food to the cemetery for the deceased.) Dad would gather dirt clods and build them into a little round "oven," start a fire within, and then, when the dirt clods were as hot as they were ever going to get and the fire had died down, would wrap up small packets of food and shove them into the little oven. He would then collapse the oven, allowing the food to bake beneath the hot clods of dirt until done.

As for the less interesting, if more functional, home oven of today (be glad you have one—until modern times, many European families had to avail themselves of the *four banal* or community oven), you can do a few things to enhance its ability to give you crisp, rustic breads. First, purchase a baking stone at a gourmet cookware store. Place it on the bottom rack of the oven and leave it there. (I bake things right on top of it all the time.) Bake your breads on the stone for an extra-special crust and thorough, even heating. Use a baker's peel or paddle dusted with cornmeal to transfer your bread to the baking stone. Second, I keep a small spray bottle full of water in the cabinet next to my oven. I spray the oven with a good mist just before putting a bread in the oven and then several times during the first 10 minutes. This approximates the steam action of a professional baker's oven and gives a crisper crust. And third, always preheat your oven for at least 20 minutes before baking to make sure it's good and hot.

Some Bread Recipes

There are a number of fabulous bread books available today, chock-full of the most mouth-watering bread recipes imaginable. Buy one. Or buy several. Read voraciously. Enjoy. But before you do that, try this: choose one or two simple recipes and make them over and over again until you are thoroughly familiar with the ins and outs of bread baking, the quirks of your own oven, the idiosyncrasies of the mixing machine you may be using, your family's likes and dislikes, and your own enthusiasm for baking bread. Then go to town on those fancy recipes.

The recipes in this chapter offer a sampling of leavening techniques, beginning with the most primitive, a simple, unleavened Indian bread called chapati. I then give recipes for a couple of yeasted breads (one using a starter and one not), and end with two recipes for breads that use chemical leavening agents.

AN UNLEAVENED BREAD

Unleavened breads or flatbreads were the earliest breads. As I mentioned before, you can find them throughout the world today, reminders of our ancestors in the days before anyone put two and two together and discovered the mysteries of leavening: tortillas in the New World, piki bread among the Hopi, chapati in India, and Mandarin pancakes in China. They are simple concoctions of flour, salt, and water and are usually baked on a grill, griddle, or hot stone.

My first lessons in making chapati came when I attended a party with a Sikh friend in Berkeley. As was the custom, the men sat in the living room, eating, talking, and drinking, while the women congregated in the kitchen and cooked! Since none of the women spoke much English, we shared an evening with the universal language: that of the kitchen, and I watched as they created a heaping platter full of hot chapati to go with a feast of Indian flavors and foods. (The flour tortilla is the next best thing to a chapati. The tortilla calls for a bit of vegetable shortening or lard added to the recipe, but is made on the same ancient principle: a dough of flour, salt, and water cooked on a hot grill.)

Chapati can be made on a medium-hot nonstick or cast iron grill surface. However, my favorite way to cook them is on the barbecue. This is the easiest and most foolproof method for cooking chapati. Steam from the quick vaporizing of the moisture in the dough causes this form of bread to rise or puff up when you put it on the grill or griddle. The chapati should puff up like a balloon within a minute or two of being put on the grill. This will ensure a light end product. If your heat is too low, the chapati will not puff and will be heavy and leaden. If you find that your chapati do not puff up on the griddle, you can place a stovetop grill or cake rack over the flame on a gas stove. A minute or two above the flame should puff the chapati nicely in addition to giving them the characteristic flecks of dark brown or black.

Chapati

Chapati is the classic flatbread of India. It is served with most meals, both as an eating utensil and as a delicious accompaniment to the spicy flavors of Indian food. The polite thing to do is to tear a piece of the chapati off in your fingers and scoop up your food with it. My kind of eating.

The traditional way to mix the dough is by hand, but I find that a food processor works very well. This quantity is a bit too small to be mixed successfully in the Magic Mill Kitchen Machine.

1½ cups unbleached
  organic bread flour
1 cup whole wheat
  bread flour
1 teaspoon salt

½ cup water (the amount
  of water you need may
  vary according to the
  kind of flour you use)

1. Blend flours and salt together in the workbowl of a food processor or by hand.

2. Add the water bit by bit until you have a soft, pliable dough in a ball or until the dough forms a ball inside the workbowl of the food processor.

3. Set the ball of dough aside to rest for 2 to 4 hours.

4. Divide the ball into eight equal pieces and roll each piece into a ball.

5. Flatten each ball with your hand, then roll into a tortilla-sized disk. Dust lightly to keep them from sticking together.

6. On a medium-hot griddle, grill, or barbecue (I use a propane gas BBQ on high), place the flat disks one by one. You will need to attend each one closely as it cooks, so set aside a plate with a towel on it for stacking the cooked chapati.

7. Each disk should puff up like a balloon, either all over or in portions, and black flecks will begin to appear on the underside. (If the chapati do not puff up on your griddle, do as I suggest above: place a cake rack over an open flame on a gas stove and, working very carefully, place a chapati on it and wait until it puffs and turns brown on each side.)

8. Lay the finished chapati on a clean towel on a plate.

Makes 8 chapati.

YEASTED BREADS

Saccharomyces cerevisiae is only one of the many strains of yeast, but it is one that is particularly dear to the hearts of humankind. It digests carbohydrates and sugars in order to live and gives off both alcohol and carbon dioxide as a result. In nature, it lives on the skins of grapes, and when the grapes are crushed, *S. cerevisiae* goes to work digesting the sugars in the grape juice. The result? A delicious alcoholic beverage we know as wine. (The carbon dioxide escapes into the air or is trapped in the bottle, as in the case of champagne.) In nature, *S. cerevisiae* also lives on grain. When the grain is crushed and mixed with water, it digests the carbohydrates in the flour and gives us carbon dioxide (which, when trapped between gluten fibers, causes dough to rise) and alcohol in small amounts, which you will smell if you leave a piece of plastic wrap tightly stretched over a bowl of sourdough starter for any length of time.

The first recipe, for Cleveland Sage Country Loaf, is a simple recipe consisting of yeast, good flour, water, salt, and a native California sage. It is very easy to make, involves a minimum investment of time, can be used as a basis for any type of herb bread, and is delicious.

The second recipe, for Green Olive Bread, involves the use of a *biga,* or Italian sourdough starter, that contains a bit of yeast, flour, and water. It, too, is delicious and will introduce you to a slightly more complex variation in the technique of making yeasted breads.

Since I have recommended the use of the Magic Mill Kitchen Machine, directions are given as if you were using it. Use the same ingredients but different techniques if you are using a Kitchen Aid, a food processor, or your own two hands.

Cleveland Sage Country Loaf

This recipe can be used as the basis for any type of herb bread, but I have chosen to pair it here with a strong, flavorful native California sage. Cleveland sage is now available at many retail nurseries or can be ordered from one of the sources listed at the end of the book. It is fairly drought resistant.

1 package yeast
  (1 tablespoon)
2 cups warm water
3 cups whole wheat
  bread flour
2 cups organic unbleached
  white bread flour

1 tablespoon salt
2 tablespoons olive oil
⅓ cup chopped fresh
  Cleveland sage leaves
Extra flour for kneading

1. Dissolve the yeast in the warm water and proof for 10 minutes. (If you own a Magic Mill Kitchen Machine, you can do this right in the mixing bowl before you add the other ingredients.)

2. Add the flours, salt, olive oil, and chopped herbs in that order to the machine and mix thoroughly.

3. Knead by machine or by hand until the dough is smooth and elastic.

4. Place the ball of dough in a bowl lightly coated with olive oil and allow it to rise, covered with a damp towel, until doubled in size (about 1½ hours).

5. Turn the dough out onto a lightly floured board and shape as you desire into two loaves.

6. Place the shaped dough on a cookie sheet or a baker's peel dusted generously with cornmeal, cover, and let rise until doubled.

7. Preheat oven to 400°F.

8. Slide one loaf onto the baking stone quickly and bake for about 45 minutes, or until it is golden on the outside and sounds hollow when tapped on its bottom. (If your oven will accommodate two loaves at the same time, you may bake them together. If not, bake one right after the other.) Be sure to mist the oven with water 3 times during the first 10 minutes of baking to ensure a crisp crust. (Use a simple plastic spray bottle filled with water.)

9. Allow the loaves to cool before cutting.

Makes 2 loaves.

Green Olive Bread

Breads made with both green and black olives, or served with green or black olives, are popular anywhere olives are grown. This simple bread is good with a chèvre cheese spread on it or served with a meal such as the one in the menu in Chapter 1.

2 teaspoons yeast	2½ to 3½ cups unbleached
2 cups warm water	white bread flour
½ cup *biga* (see recipe below)	1½ teaspoons salt
3 cups whole wheat	1½ cups chopped
bread flour	green olives

1. Dissolve the yeast in the warm water. (If you own a Magic Mill Kitchen Machine, you can do this right in the mixing bowl before you add the other ingredients.)

2. Mix in the *biga*, then the flours and salt and knead thoroughly. Mix in the chopped green olives last.

3. Oil a large mixing bowl with olive oil (again, you can let the bread rise right in the bowl of the Magic Mill) and let the bread rise, covered with a damp towel, until doubled (about 1½ hours).

4. Punch down the dough, cover the bowl again, and allow it to rise a second time until doubled (about 45 minutes the yeast organisms are really starting to "take hold").

5. Turn the dough out onto a lightly floured board and shape as you desire. (I often make this bread in two simple rustic rounds, or as rounded dinner rolls.)

6. Place the shaped dough on a cookie sheet or a baker's peel dusted generously with cornmeal and let rise until doubled. Preheat oven to 425°F.

7. Slide the risen dough quickly onto the baking stone and bake for about 45 minutes (25 minutes for rolls) or until nice and brown on the outside. (Bake both loaves together if your oven will accommodate them, or bake one right after the other.) Remove from the oven and allow it to cool before cutting (if you can!).

Makes 2 loaves.

Biga

A *biga* is really not much more than the Italian equivalent of a sourdough starter. In French, it is known as a *chef*. It requires no fancy packet of dried sourdough starter from a gourmet food store, just a technique that has been used for centuries by bakers all over the bread-baking world. Here's how you make one:

1 teaspoon active dry yeast 2 cups warm water	3½ to 4 cups flour (I use whole wheat bread flour)

Simply mix these ingredients together and let the *biga* sit for at least 24 hours to ripen. The longer the *biga* sits around at room temperature, the more sour it becomes. You can freeze any biga you don't use, and it should be perfectly good a month later if left to thaw at room temperature. You may even wish to freeze it in convenient half-cup portions.

CHEMICALLY LEAVENED BREADS

During the 19th century, Pasteur discovered that microscopic organisms were responsible for the fermentation of bread as well as of wine. To some, this seemed unhealthy, which is partly responsible for the rise in popularity of so-called quick breads. They are called quick breads because there is no extended period of waiting for the dough to rise; the leavening power is supplied by a simple chemical reaction, rather than by yeast. The mixing of an acid with an alkaline creates carbon dioxide, which causes the batter to rise. Commercial baking powders first began to appear in England in 1850.

Baking powder is the traditional leavening for that good old American standard, cornbread, and for (oddly enough) baking powder biscuits, of which the Cheddar Chive Biscuits are a variation.

Because the quantities of ingredients used here are so small, I would recommend mixing these doughs either by hand or in a food processor, rather than in the Magic Mill Kitchen Machine. Its forte is really in handling quantities of more than 4 cups of flour and in its ability to knead and mix the ingredients so efficiently.

Cornbread

There's nothing like a good, simple cornbread made with freshly ground organic corn. I always use the coarsest setting on the grain mill and the best organically grown corn I can find. This bread is wonderful all by itself. For special occasions, you might add some fresh corn, some chopped red and green (or jalapeño) peppers, or some grated sharp Cheddar cheese.

1 cup cornmeal, freshly ground	½ teaspoon baking soda
	2 tablespoons cold butter
1 cup organic unbleached pastry flour	2 eggs
	1 cup buttermilk
⅓ cup sugar	
1½ teaspoons baking powder	

1. Preheat oven to 400°F. Grease an 8-by-8-inch square baking pan. Blend the cornmeal, flour, sugar, baking powder, baking soda, and butter in the workbowl of a food processor until there are no lumps of butter left.

2. Add eggs and buttermilk, processing just until blended.

3. Pour batter into greased pan and bake for 25 minutes (or until knife or toothpick inserted in the center of the bread comes out clean).

Makes 1 8-inch-square loaf.

Cheddar Chive Biscuits

I make these biscuits with 1 cup unbleached organic all-purpose flour and 1 cup freshly ground whole wheat pastry flour. The biscuits are light yet have a nice grainy texture and flavor. They are best served hot out of the oven with a smear of grainy mustard butter, but you can also use them as a topping for chicken pot pie.

1 cup unbleached
    all-purpose flour
1 cup whole wheat
    flour (freshly ground
    if possible)
2 teaspoons baking powder
½ teaspoon baking soda

½ cup (1 stick) butter
1 cup grated sharp
    Cheddar or smoked
    Gouda cheese
¼ cup chopped
    fresh chives
⅔ cup buttermilk

1. Preheat oven to 400°F. Blend flours, baking powder, and baking soda together in the workbowl of a food processor or by hand. Mix thoroughly.

2. Add butter and process until flour has the texture of corn-meal and no lumps of butter remain.

3. Add cheese and chives and pulse just until blended.

4. Add buttermilk and pulse just until blended.

5. Remove mixture from processor and knead just long enough to bring the dough together (about a dozen turns).

6. Roll dough out about ¾ to 1 inch thick and cut into biscuits.

7. Place biscuits on oiled cookie sheet and bake for about 15 minutes (until golden brown).

Makes about 12 biscuits.

CHAPTER 7

The Fat of the Land, or How to Make Flavored Butters and Oils

THE ANCIENT WORLD seems to have been divided into two camps. On the one hand, you have your butter-eating, milk-drinking "barbarians," while on the other you have your more civilized, agrarian types, gracing their tables with (if anything) the oil of the honorable olive. Butter making most likely evolved with the nomadic peoples of the Euro-Asiatic plains (Mongols are known to have churned butter horizontally in leather pouches), from whence its consumption spread into Europe. The art of making butter was introduced to the Greeks by the Scythians (one of those Euro-Asiatic tribes), who, according to Herodotus, "poked out the eyes of their slaves so that nothing would distract them from churning their milk." Uggh. Herodotus also described the Massagetai (nomadic inhabitants of the Caucasus) as being a curious lot. "They sow no crops but live on livestock and fish, which they get in abundance . . . moreover, they are drinkers of milk." Pliny commented that butter was "considered to be the most delicate of foods among barbarous nations." Although butter was known in ancient, agrarian Greece and Rome, it was used as a healing oint-ment rather than an ingredient in cooking. On the other hand, butter was such an integral part of the lives of the nomadic

Hebrews that Abraham gave "butter and milk and the calf which he had fatted" to the three angels who visited him, and the Promised Land was referred to as a land "flowing with milk and honey"!

Although butter pops up as an incidental in various parts of Europe during the Middle Ages, we find it as a permanent fixture only in those areas that were ultimately conquered and settled by the Vikings and Normans: the Scandinavian countries, Normandy (famous for its high-quality butter), northern France, the British Isles, Iceland, and Switzerland. Its consumption appears as a force to be reckoned with only in the 14th century, when it is first mentioned by the Church in a directive on fasting. Selling abstinences to the butter-eating populations of Europe actually became a lucrative pastime for the Church, since many good, wealthy Christians were willing to pay for the privilege of eating butter during periods of abstinence. The practice so scandalized Martin Luther in 1520 that he declared, "Eating butter, they say, is a greater sin than to lie, blaspheme, or indulge in impurity." Is it a coincidence that the countries that ultimately parted ways with the Catholic Church in the 1600s were those with a history of dairy farming and butter eating?

Flavored Butters

The making of compound or flavored butters seems pretty much to be a French invention. Butter itself figures in only a small number of the recipes in France's first cookbook of importance, Taillevant's *Le Viandier* of 1380, whereas there are a whopping 21 recipes for compound butters in Escoffier's book *Le Guide Culinaire* (1903) ranging from shrimp butter (made with "shrimp remains"), to black butter (butter heated to the smoking point), to pistachio butter, to tarragon butter! Julia Child's classic, *Mastering the Art of French Cooking*, contains 10 good compound butter recipes to round out your classical repertoire.

The idea of infusing butter or fat with flavors is not a new one. Fat has been used for centuries by French perfumers to extract fragrance from delicate flowers that don't readily lend themselves to distillation. And butters are the perfect medium for melding the flavors of various and sundry herbs and then spreading them across a slab of bread or muffin.

Now don't get me wrong. I don't sit around routinely slathering butter on my morning toast. I don't even eat morning toast, and my cholesterol level is a respectable 169, but when I want to put the finishing touches on a special dinner, I'll go for butter every time.

And not just any butter. Fooling around with my herbs for a number of years has given me what I consider to be a number of winning combinations. Grilled fresh salmon with a dab of Olive Herb Butter . . . Sunday morning sourdough pancakes with Raspberry Lemon Verbena Butter . . . garlic French bread with Society Garlic Blend melted into each slice. . . all are excellent ways to perk up a jaded palate.

Making herb butter is fairly easy, and the possible flavor combinations are more numerous than the herbs in your garden. For top quality gourmet butter, you should follow a few simple tips:

- Always start with the freshest butter you can find. I use unsalted butter because its flavor is more delicate and "real" than the heavily salted variety you commonly find in the grocery store. I then have control over just how much salt (if any) is added to the finished product. (Because unsalted butter is more perishable than the salted variety, I always keep it frozen until I actually use it.)

- Make sure that any herbs or fruits used in the butter are fresh and dry. Any excess moisture will cause your butter to spoil more rapidly. You might hose off your herbs in the garden the day before you cut them. Then you don't have to wash them after they are cut.

• Try to choose herbs that complement the particular dish you have in mind, as well as each other. Use strong, earthy herbs with strong, earthy flavors (as in the Olive Herb Butter), and let the more delicate flavors play in harmony with one another.

To blend an herb butter, I use my food processor, but you can chop and mix most of them by hand if you don't have a processor. Begin with the butter at room temperature. It should be fairly soft and easily mixed. Next, add your base ingredients (those ingredients that you want thoroughly blended with the butter, such as the garlic in the Society Garlic Blend or the raspberries in the Raspberry Lemon Verbena Butter).

Once your base ingredients are thoroughly blended with the butter, you can add those ingredients that you want to have in small flecks and chunks in your butter—lemon verbena, home-cured olives, and so on. When you have achieved the color and texture you desire, you can pack and shape your butter.

Generally, you should give the flavors in a freshly made butter at least 3 or 4 hours to blend. (Overnight is better.) I usually freeze anything that I don't intend to use within a couple of days. (Herb butters can be frozen for up to three months without any significant damage to flavor.) Sometimes I pack my butters in ordinary plastic crocks, but I am more likely to do something fancy with them. Here are some ideas:

• Pack the butter into small plastic molds and freeze them until solid. Then pop each individually shaped and sized serving out into a plastic bag and keep frozen until you serve them.

• Roll the butter into fat cylinders, wrap them in freezer-weight plastic wrap, and chill until solid. Slice off rounds as needed to top vegetables, fish, bread, and so on.

• Use a pastry bag fitted with a large star tip to pipe butter florettes onto a cookie sheet. Freeze until ready to use.

• Use a butter curler to shave off colorful "curls" of herb butter.

• Make butter balls with a melon baller, then add texture with butter paddles.

• Roll the butter out to about ¾-inch thickness with a rolling pin, then use miniature cookie cutters to cut various shapes. Freeze until ready to use.

• Whip butter with a hand-held mixer until light and fluffy, then pack it in earthenware crocks.

Some Recipes for Flavored Butter

The possibilities of serving your butters attractively are numerous. You may want to play around with new ideas and combinations yourself. To get you started, here are a few of my own recipes.

Olive Herb Butter

This recipe is similar to the one for the Olive–Goat Cheese Spread in Chapter 5, but it's such a good combination of flavors that I don't see why you shouldn't enjoy it often. Use your home-cured olives (see Chapter 1) for this very flavorful butter. If you don't have any home-cured olives, use kalamata or other pungent European-type olives. The herbs can be varied to suit your taste and the contents of your herb garden at any given moment.

1 pound unsalted butter, at room temperature
2 tablespoons Dijon style mustard
2 or 3 cloves freshly pressed garlic
⅓ cup home-cured olives, pitted and chopped
2 sprigs hyssop
1 teaspoon fresh rosemary leaves
½ teaspoon fennel seed

1. Blend the butter, mustard, and garlic in a food processor until thoroughly mixed and smooth.

2. Add olives, hyssop, rosemary, and fennel seed. Blend until it reaches the desired texture.

3. Shape and refrigerate for several hours, or freeze until ready to use.

Makes about 2½ cups.

Grainy Mustard Butter

For a hearty mustard butter that can be used on the Cheddar Chive Biscuits in Chapter 6, dill bread, ham or cheese sandwiches, and probably lots of other ways, mix as much of the Basic Country-Style Mustard as you like (try 1 tablespoon for a mild mustard flavor, ¼ to ⅓ cup for a more assertive flavor) with a pound of butter at room temperature. Shape and refrigerate or freeze until ready to use.

Raspberry–Lemon Verbena Butter

Lemon verbena is a shrub native to South America. It drops its leaves in the winter but in the spring and summer produces incredibly fragrant, lemon-flavored leaves that are used in both cooking and perfumery. It makes an excellent butter when used in combination with either strawberries or raspberries.

1 pound unsalted butter, at room temperature
2 tablespoons sugar (or to taste)
8 ounces fresh or frozen raspberries (not in syrup)

Handful of lemon verbena leaves (use young, tender leaves, stripped of their veins)

1. Blend the butter, sugar, and raspberries in a food processor until quite smooth and emulsified. Please note: *this will appear impossible at first.* Just persist. The fruit and butter will eventually emulsify into a beautiful, sweet, pink mass.

2. Add the lemon verbena leaves (strip out any large veins) and let the machine run until the leaves are chopped to suit you.

3. Shape and refrigerate or freeze until ready to use.

Makes about 3 cups.

Society Garlic Blend

This wonderful butter has a strong garlic butter base with the pale lavender blossoms of society garlic (*Tulbaghia violacea*; see Chapter 2) and green chives blended in for color, texture, and flavor accent.

1 pound unsalted
   butter, at room
   temperature
3 large cloves (or more)
   pressed fresh garlic

½ cup society garlic
   blossoms
¼ cup chopped fresh chives

1. Thoroughly blend the butter and garlic in the food processor.
2. Add the society garlic flowers and chopped chives, and blend until it reaches the desired texture.
3. Shape and refrigerate or freeze until ready to use.

Makes about 2¼ cups.

Rosemary Orange Butter

Not everyone realizes that the blossoms of most herbs are just as edible as the leaves, and they are a heck of a lot more colorful. Use this butter on a whole-grain bread, your favorite muffins, or on slices of orange cake.

1 pound unsalted
   butter, at room
   temperature
1 tablespoon chopped
   fresh rosemary leaves

1 to 2 tablespoons
   rosemary blossoms
1 teaspoon freshly
   grated orange zest

1. Blend all ingredients in a food processor until the desired texture is reached.
2. Shape and refrigerate or freeze until ready to use.

Makes about 2¼ cups.

Flavored Oils

Oils are the "butter" of the agrarian people of the Mediterranean lands. Ancient Egyptians favored sesame seed, flaxseed, and even radish seed oils, while the Greeks and most of the rest of the Mediterranean world favored the oil of the sacred olive tree. Asian peoples relied upon soy and coconut oils, while peanut, corn, and sunflowers supplied oil to the inhabitants of the Americas. Methods of extraction varied somewhat from culture to culture and oil to oil, but the basic idea remained the same. You crushed the seed or nut, squashed the oil and juices out of it (or sometimes boiled the oil and juices out of it), waited for the oil to rise to the top, and then scooped it off.

Oils and fats act as solvents for the aromatic essences in plant matter. This principle has been called upon in medicine, ritual, and perfumery for centuries. The ancient Egyptians used to anoint themselves with perfumed oils. Yahweh taught Moses to make an anointing oil of myrrh, cinnamon, and cassia with a "hin" (whatever that is) of olive oil (Exodus 30), while modern-day rural Mexicans make an excellent balm for sore muscles by soaking rue or marijuana in oil. However, a survey of ancient through modern cooking and food literature will show that although oils have been used for cooking since ancient times, the idea of flavoring oils with herbs and spices is pretty much a 20th century innovation, at least insofar as the culinary arts are concerned. My theory is that until relatively recently, methods of filtering and refining oils have been primitive at best, meaning that most oils used in cooking around the world have resembled what we can purchase today in health food stores as unrefined oil. I love unrefined oil; it is full of flavor and aroma, with minuscule particles of plant matter suspended in the liquid. However, in most cases, the oil itself is so strongly aromatic that I think no additional flavoring was deemed necessary or desirable by most cultures.

I can think of only a few cases in which flavored oils are

found even in traditional Mediterranean dishes today. The *bagna cauda* of southern France and northern Italy is a tribute to the first press of the olive. Oil is heated in a sort of chafing dish, then garlic, butter, and anchovies are added to flavor the already pungent brew. Fresh, raw vegetables are then dipped in the "soup" and devoured enthusiastically by the whole family. Pesto (Liguria) or pistou (Provence) is more properly a sauce made largely from oil, basil, Parmesan cheese, and garlic, though I'm not sure I'd consider it a flavored oil per se. Aside from these two readily available examples, oil is oil and herbs or other flavorings are just that. And making "flavored" or "herb" oils for culinary purposes remains a fairly contemporary practice.

Some Recipes for Flavored Oils

Making flavored oils is similar to making flavored vinegars. They are a terrific medium in which to preserve the summer garden. Flavored oils can enhance your cooking in any number of ways. They can be used in marinades, salad dressings, and sauces.

The type of oil you use will depend upon the effect you want to achieve. Olive oil offers an excellent base when a hearty and flavorful effect is needed. For those dishes that require something a little more subtle, use canola oil. Like olive oil, it is monounsaturated (which means it may help to lower elevated cholesterol levels). When a delicate flavor is required, you might try walnut oil (which, unfortunately, goes rancid rather quickly) or sunflower seed oil. If at all possible, try to obtain oils that have been produced without the use of pesticides and insecticides.

The traditional method for infusing oils with herb flavors is the same as that used for making herb vinegars: choose a suitable combination of herbs or spices, fill a jar with them, pour in some oil, and let the mixture sit at room temperature until the oil has reached the strength you desire. Make sure the jar is tightly capped and filled nearly to the rim to exclude oxygen and prevent the oil from going rancid. When the oil has reached the desired intensity of flavor, strain it and bottle it. Add a "cosmetic" sprig of herb or a little whole spice, always making sure any plant matter you add is perfectly dry before adding it to the oil.

Basil Oil

This method of making basil oil produces a bright green, highly flavored, thick oil that will keep its flavor and color for months if refrigerated in tightly capped, well-filled bottles. It is not recommended for cooking, but for drizzling on top of a tomato/ mozzarella salad, fresh green beans, or anything else where its visual appearance will make an impression and its fresh flavor will be appreciated. Mayonnaise made from this oil has a pretty green color and an intense flavor. The pinch of ascorbic acid is added as an antioxidant (remember that oxygen accelerates rancidity of oil and decay of plant matter).

This oil can be made with almost any type of fresh herb and is particularly attractive when made with purple opal basil.

A large bunch of fresh
basil (about as much
as 2 bunches of spinach)

1 cup olive oil
Pinch of ascorbic acid

1. Blanch the basil in boiling water for about 10 seconds. (This stops the enzymatic action, which would contribute to its decay.)

2. Squeeze all the moisture you can out of the basil. Wring it out as you might a dishcloth.

3. Place ½ cup of the oil, the basil, and the pinch of ascorbic acid in a blender. Blend until emulsified. Add the rest of the oil and blend again.

4. Strain through a sieve or fine-mesh strainer, bottle (filling bottles with as much oil as possible), and store in the refrigerator.

Makes about 2 cups.

Hazelnut Oil

To create a unique oil full of fresh, nutty flavor and texture, this recipe uses both hazelnut butter and ground, freshly roasted hazelnuts. I suggest you roast and grind your hazelnuts just before using them for freshest results. Remember that nut oils and butters go rancid fairly quickly, so you will want to store any unused oil tightly capped in the refrigerator.

Health food stores usually carry various types of nut butters. Be sure to buy small quantities and store the nut butters in the refrigerator, since they are fragile and can become rancid quickly. This nut oil can be made with any number of different nuts, depending upon the need of the moment: walnuts, cashews, almonds, peanuts, and so on.

1 cup hazelnuts
1 tablespoon hazelnut
   butter

1 cup hazelnut or
   canola oil

1. Preheat oven to 325°F. Place the hazelnuts in a pie plate or on a cookie sheet and toast them for about 10 minutes or until lightly browned and aromatic. (This is a good way to bring out the flavor in any kind of nut or spice.)

2. Grind the toasted nuts in either a coffee mill or a food processor, being sure to leave some texture.

3. Blend the hazelnut oil and the hazelnut butter together in a blender.

4. Add the ground, toasted hazelnuts and blend until mixed. Use shortly after making and store any excess in a tightly capped, well-filled bottle in the refrigerator.

Makes about 2 cups.

Patti's Industrial-Strength Garlic Spread

This is my favorite recipe for an herb and oil "quickie." It's positively deadly.

1 cup olive oil (or canola oil)	Tons of assorted fresh herbs, such as chives,
½ cup peeled fresh garlic cloves	tarragon, basil, thyme, parsley, marjoram, and the inner leaves of celery

Mix the ingredients thoroughly in a blender. I like to stop blending when the herbs and garlic are in reasonable pieces rather than blending them to a pulp. Spread on freshly baked bread, or spread on French bread and heat until piping hot.

Note: The Department of Agriculture now suggests that you not store garlic in olive oil for any extended period of time because of the remote danger of botulinum spores proliferating. If you must store it, add some vinegar to boost its acid content, or freeze it. Best is to eat it all at one sitting!

Makes about 1½ cups.

Sources

HERB PLANTS & SEEDS

River Ridge Farms
(live plants)
3135 West Los Angeles Avenue
Oxnard, CA 93030
(805) 647-6880

Herban Gardens (live plants)
5002 Second Street
Rainbow, CA 92028
(619) 723-2967

Nichols Garden Nursery
(saffron crocus, seeds, and
live plants)
1190 N. Pacific Highway
Albany, OR 94321-4598
(503) 928-9280

Seeds Blum (saffron crocus,
herb, and specialty veggie seeds)
Idaho City Stage
Boise, ID 83707
No phone business.

Shepherd's Garden Seeds
(herb, flower, and specialty
veggie seeds)
30 Irene Street
Torrington, CT 06790-6627
(203) 482-3638

*River Ridge Farms and Herban
Gardens deal in live plants only.
Seeds Blum, Shepherd's Garden
Seeds, and Nichols Garden Nursery
all offer a host of herb, vegetable,
and flower seeds, good books, and
garden equipment.*

MUSTARD SEEDS & SUPPLIES

**Mount Horeb
Mustard Museum**
109 East Main Street
Mount Horeb, WI 53572
(800) 438-6878

The Mount Horeb Mustard Museum sells whole and cracked brown and yellow mustard seed at very reasonable prices, as well as books on making and using mustard, and publishes an amusing biannual newsletter called *The Proper Mustard*. Their large volume of business with rapid turnover insures a fresh product!

VINEGAR-MAKING SUPPLIES

Beer and Wine Craft
450 Fletcher Parkway
El Cajon, CA 92020
(619) 447-9191

Great Fermentations
87 Larkspur Street
San Rafael, CA 94901
(800) 570-2337

Milan Home Brew Shop
57 Spring Street
New York, NY 10012
(800) 233-7534

Barrel Builders
P.O. Box 268
St. Helena, CA 94574
(800) 365-8231

Barrel Builders specializes in oak barrels for the wine trade and carries a lovely selection of plain and carved vinegar-sized barrels. Milan Home Brew Shop carries vinegar-making kits. Beer and Wine Craft and Great Fermentations both carry a fairly complete line of unpasteurized vinegar, barrels, and related equipment.

CHEESEMAKING SUPPLIES

**New England Cheese-
making Supply Company**
Box 85
Ashfield, MA 01330-0085
(413) 628-3808

The New England Cheesemaking Supply Company carries a good selection of books, cultures, cheese molds, and other equipment for making cheeses.

WHOLE GRAINS & GRAIN MILLS

Shipping costs for grain are often prohibitive, so if you expect to purchase grain in large amounts, I recommend ordering them through your local health food store. That way, they pay the shipping charges.

**Nutriflex/Magic Mill
Corporation**
P.O. Box 45115
Salt Lake City, UT 84145
(800) 888-8587

Call the Nutriflex/Magic Mill Corporation for the name of a sales representative in your area. The company does not sell direct to the public.

Walnut Acres

Penns Creek, PA 17862

(800) 433-3998

Walnut Acres charges a flat $4.90 shipping fee for its 25-pound bags of grain. It offers both hard and soft wheat along with a host of milled flours.

King Arthur Flour

P.O. Box 876

Norwich, VT 05055-0876

(800) 777-4434

King Arthur Flour offers flour and wheat in small quantities, along with a very nice selection of books and bread-baking equipment. Baking is their business.

Pamela's Products

156 Utah Avenue

South San Francisco, CA 94080

(415) 952-4546

Pamela runs a retail mail order business in conjunction with Giusto's, a supplier of quality grains to the trade. She offers a complete line of flours and whole grains. Her shipping costs are fairly high.

About the Author

LYNN ALLEY was born and raised in the San Francisco Bay Area. She graduated from the University of California, Berkeley, with a degree in English Literature and attended graduate school at a small private college in Marin County. After graduating, she went to live in England, where she studied herbal medicine. Frequent vacations in France hooked her on good food and fresh ingredients.

Upon her return to the United States, Alley moved to southern California and took up teaching. She specializes in cooking with and cultivating fresh herbs. Alley conducted culinary tours and lunches at the largest herb nursery in the United States and has taught classes on cooking and vinegar making at the Robert Mondavi Food and Wine Education Center in Costa Mesa, California, and at several Williams-Sonoma locations throughout southern California. She has contributed articles on cooking and herbs to the *Herb Companion Magazine, Cook's Illustrated*, and *The San Diego Tribune*. She currently writes and edits a newsletter for a wholesale specialty herb and vegetable nursery in southern California. Alley lives today in Carlsbad, California, with her husband, three cats, a rabbit, and numerous herbs and fruit trees. This is her first book.